BEYOND CLASSIFICATION: BOOK NUMBERS

BEYOND CLASSIFICATION: BOOK NUMBERS

With Special Reference to Chronological Book Numbers

Mohinder Partap Satija

and

John P. Comaromi

Ess Ess Publications

4837/24, ANSARI ROAD, DARYA GANJ
NEW DELHI-110002
Phone : 3260807

First Published 1992

ISBN: 81-7000-136-6

RS. 400

Published by
Sheel Sethi (Mrs.) *for*
Ess Ess Publications
Ansari Road, Daryaganj
New Delhi-110 002.

Composed at
DTP & Allied Services
A-245, Majlis Park, Azadpur, Delhi-110 033

Printed by: **Novelty Process.**
E-4/1, Mansrover Park, Delhi-110 032.

Dedicated to

Professor Ken Bakewell

and

Jens B. Friis–Hansen

Contents

Preface

> We are truly heirs of all the ages; but as honest men it behooves us to learn the extent of our inheritance and as brave ones not to whimper if it should prove less than what we had supposed.
>
> Anonymous

Book numbers have only a subsidiary function in the process of library classification. Because of this classificationists have shied away from writing on the subject, and practitioners have probably never given serious consideration to them. Consequently, book numbers face several crises: a crisis of definition, of identity, of status, and of survival as an academic subject. Book numbers, though coeval with the relative classification that was advanced by Melvil Dewey, seems to have attained quickly a state of saturated interest, whereas subject classification is always opening its windows to new vistas. Perhaps to the current generation of librarians book numbers appears to be too primitive and old-fashioned a subject to yield professional dividends. Perhaps it is that to the professionals talking in information jargon the *book* number represents a retrogade step. Whatever the case, the subject finds few scholars to consider it. Standard textbooks on classification no longer devote respectable space to book numbers. Our major reference tool the *Encyclopedia of Library and Information Science* only recently included an article on book numbers. Indeed, to this very day only two pamphlets and two books have been published on book numbers: the pamphlets: Anna Cantrell Laws, *Author Notation in the Library of Congress*, Washington, D.C., GPO, 1917; 18p.; and Bertha Barden.*Book Numbers: a Manual for Students with a Basic Code of Rules*, Chicago, American Library Association, 1937; 31p.; and the books: Donald J. Lehnus, *Book Numbers: History, Principles, and Application*, Chicago, American Library Association, 1980; and John P. Comaromi, *Book Numbers: a Historical Study and Practical Guide to Their Use*, Littleton, Colo., Libraries Unlimited, 1981. Current periodical literature of much worth is no longer to be found.

There is no continuity in the literature on the four systems described in the text that follows; one belongs to the 19th century, the rest to the 20th. Nor can one perceive a developing line of thought in them. S. R. Ranganathan described in passing many book number systems in his *Prolegomena.* It is unlikely that he did not know of Brown's Chronological system while settling on the nature of his own book number system. His debt to Biscoe is obvious. Nevertheless, a continuing line of thought is not provable.

The present work has been prompted by the two books on book numbers. These monographs, as scholarly as they are, have only studied and described book numbers in American libraries; they ignored the world beyond. This book seeks to complement these works by devoting itself to chronological book numbers—a mostly ignored rival line to alphabetical book numbers, indeed an ignored aspect of an ignored subject. The first four chapters dwell upon the theoretical and general problems of book numbers: their definition, nature, usefulness, and history. The chapter on the debate over the usefulness of book numbers tries to give the reader a taste of the debate that followed their conception and immediate development. Chapter four enumerates the advantages of using chronological book numbers. The remaining four chapters dwell upon the four specific chronological book numbering systems. The description of each system is prefaced by a brief life sketch of the inventor. Ranganathan's system has been fully, but concisely, explained. His system, though often written about in India, is not well known nor used outside its shores.

This book is not a manual; many practical problems have been left unexamined. It is not an edifice, but is a scaffold for further future work. It does aim to invite the attention of scholars to a neglected part of our heritage to give it a fair trial and from the trial a measure of its efficacy. Moreover, this work will serve to prompt us to reconsider the role and form of book numbers in the fast-coming era of automated storage and retrieval systems and the paperless society—a job just begun by Karen Markey Drabenstott of the University of Michigan.

Mohinder Partap Satija
John P. Comaromi

Acknowledgments

It is a pleasant duty to acknowledge the help and material received in producing this work. Thanks to the Library Association (London) for the material on James Duff Brown; to the American Library Association for material on Walter Stanley Biscoe; to Olin Library, Wesleyan University; to May Zinda (daughter of W.S. Merrill) for the material on the life of her father; and to the University of Wyoming in Laramie and to the Oconomowoc Public Library for source material on W.S. Merrill. Thanks also to Ken Bakewell for his comments on the first draft of the work.

CHAPTER 1

Book Numbers: Introduction

Knowledge is ephemeral until and unless it is embodied in a concrete form without which it cannot be preserved or propagated. Documents record knowledge. Though the nature and physical shape of documents have changed with the technological state of society, the documents have always remained a major means to record, preserve, and disseminate knowledge. Access to knowledge is the librarian's stock-in-trade, but we deal with knowledge only as embodied in documents. The relation between knowledge and the document recording it is that of soul and body. Modern library classification is basically knowledge classification, but inevitably the realities and peculiarities of the physical body of the document cannot be ignored in the organization of a library.

It is generally accepted that a class number alone, howsoever minute it be, fails to individualize a book on the shelf or in a bibliography. Many books in a library get the same class number by virtue of having the same specific subject. Class numbers alone produce groupings whose size depends upon the depth of the library classification and the closeness with which the classification used is applied. To organize or provide order within a class grouping, documents are given a further notation called a *book number.* As the book number is based on some external characteristic of the document (that is to say, the characteristic does not deal with the subject of the document), the notation used in the book number is also known as *external notation.* Book numbers may be based on one or a combination of some of the attributes of the document, such as author, title, language, year or place of publication, physical size, and physical make-up. The book number may also reflect such characteristics as volume number, copy number, whether the document is a supplement or commentary (which serves to bring together a core document and its related documents). The role of a book number begins where that of the class number ends. Thus the class number and the book number are respectively two consecutive steps in library organization. Together they constitute the *call number* that provides a unique and individualizing address so that a document can be found in its physical location associated with the relatives of the subject content of a document. In short, book numbers mean a step beyond (subject) classification: it is classification within classification.

Broadly speaking and currently, there are two prevalent systems of book numbers. The older and the still far more popular system is to subarrange alphabetically by author—strictly speaking, by the heading under which the document is catalogued. In this system the author's name is converted into a decimal fraction preceded by the initial letter of the author's surname or the heading, e.g., Ranganathan R196, Ireland I65. This number is called the *cutter number* regardless whether the number has been taken from a table devised by Charles Ammi Cutter. Many versions of cutter tables and other such systems are available now. The other approach is to subarrange documents within a class by the year of their publication. In such a case, the year of publication is converted into a notation briefer than the year itself made up usually of a letter of the alphabet followed by decimal digits, e.g., W9 or K9 or N69 for 1969.

Till recently the term "book number" succinctly defined the notation used for subarranging documents within a given specific class. Some have come to challenge the term as the word "book" may be seen to exclude nonbook material—which is now pouring into our libraries. However, the terms *author number* or *author mark* exclude the idea of arrangement by year of publication. And all alphabetical subarrangements are not by author: some are by title and some by geographical place name. Moreover, "author number" may suggest the exclusion of the work mark and other facets in a book number. The author number is a central part of the alphabetical book number, but it is not the only part. Many suggest "cutter number" as a substitute for book number.[1] Indeed, over the years "cuttering" has been accepted as a verb in the English language that indicates alphabetical subarrangement. Unfortunately it is not restricted to the book number; it is used to indicate subject as well.

A more apt term (though one less appealing) is "external notation." John P. Comaromi writes:

> External notation is also called author numbers or book numbers....One often encounters the phrase "Cutter numbers" when dealing with the LCC and when shelflisting for it. Like "book numbers" it is an umbrella phrase. Unlike it, however, it has a significance considerably beyond its usual meaning. "Cutter numbers" may refer to the elements of the class number in which subjects are represented by the cutter number. Cuttering is done for subjects, authors, and for many other useful groupings. Be advised, then, that a cutter number may be something other than a book number, and that cuttering is a process wherein an initial letter followed by an arabic numeral or numerals used as [like] decimal fractions represent the rest of the name regardless of whether the name is a subject, author, title, or anything else.[2]

The term "shelflisting" is perhaps most useful as it means the process of subarranging the class numbers of a library; at least, that is what the term means in the *Library of Congress Subject Headings*. It applies to preparing items for the shelf, not merely preparing the *shelflist* (the catalog of the holdings of a libary in the order the material is found on the shelves). Well, this is all a confusion of terms, a confusion that afflicts many areas of librarianship but is not peculiar to librarianship. The functions of book numbers are quite clear and understod; that is what matters.

In the art of library shelf organization the first grouping of books does not take into consideration the subject matter. The first consideration is the section to which the document should go. We first determine whether the document under classification is a rare book, a manuscript, a thesis, a reference book, or any sort of special collection book. One of us [John Comaromi] was once a circulation librarian at a college library having some 70,000 volumes. It fell to him to house in his office the Star Collection (a star was placed upon the spine of each item in the Collection). Here were kept those items in danger of being stolen or mutilated: books with racy passages, those on birth control, and those art works with removable plates were some of the major categories.) These sections may be dictated by a utilitarian purpose, such as reference, or for the convenience of managing them, such as oversized books, rare books, and so on. Thus in a library there are found many mini-libraries.

The symbol indicating the section of the library in which the document is to be housed is called the *collection number;* it usually precedes immediately the classification number. Putting the symbol for the collection number seems so simple and obvious an act that it seems no scheme other than the Colon Classification has discussed it in an academic way. (In CC the collection number has been designed in relation to the book number.) In most situations a separate symbol is added for the collection number. It may be any arbitrary symbol, but it is usually the initial letter of the name of the section of the library:

R Reference
RR Rare book
T Thesis
G Government publication
RP Reports.

If it is a departmental library, Ranganathan suggested the following convention:

BD Mathematics Department
LD Medical College
YD Sociology Department
ZD Law School

But for unusual books Ranganathan enumerated the following rules:

Underline the book number for small-sized books
Overline the book number for large-sized books
Both overline and underline the book number for unusual books
Encircle the book number for worn out books.[3]

One wonders why Ranganathan did not discard worn out books.

Since each symbol creates its own section, no ordinal value of the symbols has been fixed. The sections are located with respect to convenience, nothing else. The general collection is not given a collection symbol, which is an application of the favoured category principle.

The combination of collection number, class number, and book number when taken together in the given sequence is termed the call number (already mentioned above with respect to the general collection). It is the call number that provides an address for the location of an item in a library. By equation it is: Call number = Collection number + Class number + Book number. In actual practice the collection number is usually written first followed by the class number on the line below it. The book number follows the class number on the same line (with a gap of two spaces or less) or it is written below the class number, e.g.:

Ref
611 for *Gray's Anatomy*
G77

References

1. Wynar, Bohdan S. *Introduction to Cataloging and Classification*. 7th edition by Arlene G. Taylor; Littleton, Colo.: Libraries Unlimited, 1985; p. 426
2. Comaromi, John P. *Book Numbers*. Littleton, Colo.; Libraries Unlimited, 1981; p. 118
3. Ranganathan, S.R. Colon Classification. 6th edition; Bombay: Asia Publishing House, 1963; Sec. 043 (p. 1.18)

CHAPTER 2

Debate over the Usefulness of Book Numbers

> "...to pay scant attention to shelf listing [book numbers] is to leave the frosting off the cake. The cake can be eaten, to be sure, but with less ease and appreciation"—John Comaromi

Book numbers are viewed by many as being little more than optional adjuncts to bibliographic classification. Their aim, however, is the complete individualization of a book on the shelf. We understand that the usefulness of minute classification is still doubted by many; these same people take book numbers to be unnecessary. They assume that in a closely classified library (one using depth classification) or in a small library, book numbers may be safely dispensed with. Even the stout Margaret Mann argued that "the number of books in any one class would not be great enough to cause confusion even if these were not in exact order."[1] Susan Grey Akers quoted A.E. Markley as having said that "a general library with up to 50,000 volumes can do without book numbers"; and also referred to Margaret Nicholson, who believed "that book numbers are not necessary in any school library".[2] Margaret Mann believed further that "some libraries feel that book numbers are altogether superfluous; that while exact order may not always be maintained on the shelves, especially where readers have direct access to the books, this inconvenience is slight compared to the work involved in assigning them".[3] Mann went on that "the point is also made that time is saved when the book number is not written on book cards, catalog cards, and other records". All these arguments can be traced to Bertha Barden, who also maintained that in open-access libraries readers will most of the time go directly to the shelves to locate their documents rather than try to find them through the catalog. For which reason, she argued, the utility of book numbers is lessened.[4] W.H. Phillip's elaborate argument against book numbers may be summarized as follows:

(1) it is a relatively complicated tool for a relatively simple process, one that makes the notation more complicated

(2) such numbers are only approximate in their achievement (even in a minute and precise author table that enumerates all names, it may not be able to arrange further by the author's initials. So all Smiths will get mixed regardless of their forenames)

(3) author numbers unnecessarily mystify an author's name when it it is easily understandable as such

(4) the author's name usually appears on the spine of a book, and this can be used as the book number.[5]

James Duff Brown (who himself devised two systems of book numbers, one an author table and the other a chronological table) preferred to subarrange books by the authors' names as they appeared *on the book* rather than to convert them to any code.[6] Ranganathan quoted that very Brown: "Perhaps the most sensible and straightforward way to distinguish books from each other is to rely entirely upon the class number or symbol, plus the lettering on the books themselves".[8]

Some of the above arguments indeed have merit, that is why some libraries do not use book numbers, while others simply use one, two, or three of the initial letters of the author's surname for subarranging books within the same class.

On the other side of the coin, several important library thinkers held and hold opposite views. H.E. Bliss (though he himself devised no book number system) argued that the lack of a book number in the call number made the location of a book very "difficult, slow, and uncertain".[7] Ranganathan not only preferred and advocated a systematic method of providing book numbers, he made their provision statutory in a scheme of classification by enunciating the Canon of the book number in his *Prolegomena:* "A scheme for classification should include a scheme for book numbers in order to individualise the documents having the same subject as their ultimate class and to mechanise their preferred arrangement among themselves".[8] If the Canon is followed, then *ad hoc* book numbers can be replaced by systematic ones. And when a classification scheme designs its own book numbers, the relation between book number and class number will be intrinsic and complementary. Melvil Dewey found book numbers to be necessary so that "books may be quickly and accurately placed, called for, found, and charged".[9] W.S. Biscoe, Dewey's lieutenant, urged a very minute classification to reduce the quantity of books under each class number.[10] But that by no means obviated the need for book numbers.

Somehow, the idea has insinuated itself into librarians' minds that the more minute a classification, the less the need for book numbers. Donald Lehnus was right when he concluded that "if there are only a few items with the same classification number, the book number can be simple, but if the library has many items classified under one number, then it must be more detailed".[11] Lehnus advised that book numbers are relative. In essence it boils down to the old argument that if the library is small, the classification may be broader; but classification has, of necessity, to be minute when the library grows in collection. Without book numbers there will be pockets of chaos under every class number. John Comaromi warned that without book numbers the cost of retrieving documents will be burdensome and even frustrating to both reader and staff. With cogent argument he showed that no-book-number policy will exhaust the patience of users.[12]

Susan Grey Akers quoted Bertha Barden, the first major writer on book numbers, on six uses of them:

(1) to arrange books in order on the shelves
(2) to provide a brief and accurate call number for each book
(3) to locate a particular book on the shelf
(4) to provide a symbol for charging books to borrow
(5) to facilitate the return of books to the shelves
(6) to assist in quick identification of a book when inventories are taken[14]

Beyond all this, book numbers may form a facet of a class number where further characteristics of division are arranged alphabetical by name. That is, to work as an Alphabetical Device (in Ranganathan's terminology) even though Ranganathan did not use book numbers for this purpose. The Library of Congress Classification employs the device so often that one would think it owned the idea. And LCC numbers frequently have several book numbers at a time.

In some classes, such as fiction and biography, book numbers play an enormous role in organizing the subject of the work. Book numbers are also used to arrange reports, files, and other records in libraries and archives.

For those who abandon book numbers to "save time" Margaret Mann advised "that the time saved by the catalog department in not assigning them [book numbers] is more than offset by the hours lost in hunting for books misplaced on the shelves and by the inconvenience of having no complete symbol for the charging system and other records". She continued: "The reader, who has little time to copy authors and titles and specify editions, usually appreciates call numbers. He has a far better chance of getting what he asks for."[15] She also reported that some librarians that had discarded book numbers for nonfiction found the result to be quite unsatisfactory; they returned to the use of book numbers.[16] Her findings have been corroborated by J. Holock from his experience in Danish libraries that had abolished book numbers. He showed that the time saved in not giving book numbers is not true timesaving in the end.[17] Moreover, there can be no efficient shelf list without book numbers; and the numerous uses to which a shelf list is put are obvious. The uses of a classified catalog for a research library are common knowledge; without book numbers a classified catalog cannot be organized effectively.

The opponents of book numbers are probably as much spurred by inertia as by anything else to prompt them not to use book numbers. At bottom, humanity is lazy; unfortunately it sets its laziness upon the backs of the next generation.

References

1. Mann, Margaret. *Introduction to Cataloging and Classification of Books*. 2nd ed. Chicago: ALA, 1943 (1971 reprint); p. 88
2. Akers, Susan Grey. *Simple Library Cataloging*. 5th ed. Metuchen, N.J.: Scarecrow Press, 1969; p. 32
3. Mann, Margaret. *Op. Cit.* p. 88
4. Barden, Bertha R. *Book Numbers*. Chicago: ALA, 1937; p. 10
5. Phillips, W. Howard. *A Primer of Book Classification*. Rev. ėd. London: Association of Assistant Librarians, 1951; pp. 54-55
6. Brown, James Duff. *Subject Classification*. 3rd ed., rev. by J.D. Stewart. London: Grafton, 1939; p. 27
7. Bliss, Henry E. *Organization of Knowledge in Libraries*. New York: H.W. Wilson, 1939; p. 68

8. Ranganathan, S.R. *Prolegomena to Library Classification*. 3rd ed. Bombay: Asia, 1967; Sec. UB2, p. 503
9. Dewey, Melvil. *Simplified Library School Rules: Card Catalogs, Accession, Book Numbers, Shelfist, Capitals, Punctuation, Abbreviations, Library Handwriting*. Boston: Library Bureau, 1898: p. 53.
10. Lehnus, Donald J. *Book Numbers*. Chicago: ALA, 1980; p. 23
11. *Ibid.* p. 75
12. Comaromi, John P. *Book Numbers*. Littleton, Colo.: Libraries Unlimited, 1981; p. 11
13. Akers, Susan Grey. *Op. cit.* p. 32
14. Barden, Bertha R. *Op. cit.* p. 9
15. Mann, Margaret. *Op. cit.* p. 88
16. *Ibid.* p. 89
17. Holock, J. "Om afskaffelse of forfattermaeker" [About the Doing Away with Author Numbers], *Bibliotekaren* 19(1), 1957:1-4

CHAPTER 3

History of Book Numbers

Book numbers are an adjunct to the class numbers of a relative classification—a family sired by melvil Dewey in 1873. In the pre-Dewey days of fixed location systems, book numbers were not needed. Inevitably, the origin and development of book numbers is coeval with the development of the relative classification systems, though independent of them. At Amherst College (where Dewey devised his Decimal Classification) Dewey had tried placing the author's name in full, or abbreviated, form after the class number:

575		575
	or	
Darwin		Dar

The alphabet below the class number represented the book number. This primitive method was soon found to be unwieldy. Dewey then decided to use the simplest of all possible methods: numbering each book in a class according to its accession in the library. "Thus 160.1 would be the first book on logic, 160.2 the second".[1] (It may be reminded here that in the first edition of the DDC, no decimal point was used in the class number. It was assumed to stand *before* the first digit of the class number.) The dot used between the class number and the accession number was raised a bit above the base line. Hence this raised "decimal point" was used as a signpost between the class number and the book number.

Even at that late date in the 19th century, the size of a book was an important consideration in shelf arrangement. If the book was of abnormal size, the size number was added between the class and book numbers. For example, in 160.4.17, 160 is the class number, 4 means the quarto size (24x30 cm), and 17 is the book number for the seventeenth quarto in class 160. So, within a given class the books were first arranged by size and then further subarrnaged by order of accession within that size. Such a method promoted both the saving of space and aesthetic qualities. However, browsing was disjoined and space was soon to become a minor factor in library planning in the United States. The method was doomed to the brief life it deserved.

At the beginning, the accession number method was considered quite satisfactory. But Dewey caught on quickly to its shortcomings:

> (1) The author, date, publisher, language, style of treatment are entirely disregarded and only an accession order exists
> (2) There is no way to locate a specific book except to know its precise number, while Cutter numbers arrange them by author.[2]

In the early 1880s many systems of book numbers were experimented with, advocated, tried, and discarded. The method of book numbers that was to become most popular had its antecedents prior to even 1876, though the origin of book numbers in the real sense is traced back to the year 1878.[3] As early as 1872 Jacob Schwartz (1846-1926), Librarian of the New York Aprrentices' Library from 1871 to 1900, arranged alphabetically all the sections of his library. He devised a table to convert an author's name into number. Its mechanism consisted in assigning integral numbers 1-99 to a combination of letters. This "Combined System" was able to generate 6500 classes and subclasses by combining A-Z, 1-9, and a-z. His system also took account of the book size and, consequently, arranged books by size and author simultaneously within a given class.

Schwartz created two author tables. His second table, part of his Mnemonic Classification, was published in 1882.[4] According to Lehnus, "This table had a dual purpose; it was an author table and also served to further subdivide each basic classification".[5] Happily, both tables are constructed on scientific principles regarding the frequency of occurrence of personal names within various letters. As an aside: Comaromi said of Schwartz that "he might have risen in the library profession to a respected position had he not possessed a mordant sense of humor and an impudent tongue. As it was, after several bitter disputes he disappeared from library history".[6]

Charles Ammi Cutter preferred Schwartz's alphabetical book numbers over Dewey's accession number method. He made a fundamental and lasting improvement in book numbers when in 1878 he proposed to treat the numerical portion of a book number as a decimal fraction—he being greatly taken by Dewey's use of decimal fractions in the recently published Decimal Classification. Cutter seems to have been the first to advocate less emphasis on book size in book numbers. His advocacy in this regard was important in the metamorphosis that led to Dewey's saying that subarrangement by size was utter nonsense. It is amazing how a practice can one day be avowed and the next utter nonsense.

The latter 1870s was a hectic period in the history of book numbers. Their golden age was long past by the end of the nineteenth century. Many new and varied book numbering ideas swarmed in the literature of the time. In its February, 1879, issue the then young *Library Journal* published a symposium on book numbers, to which several of the leading librarians of the day submitted their thought. Among them were Dewey, Cutter, Josephus Nelson Larned (Librarian of the young Men's Association of Buffalo—and the man who put the decimal point in the Decimal Classification), John Edmands (Librarian of the Philadelphia Mercantile Library), and John Fitzpatrick (Librarian of the Bronson Library of Waterbury, Connecticut).[7] In the symposium John Edmands (1820-1915) added another facet to book numbers by suggesting that the initial letter of the author's surname should be prefixed to the decimal number standing for the author's name. At first, Cutter objected to Edmands' ideal of mixing letters and numbers. He preferred alphabets for class numbers and numbers for book numbers. Later, however, he changed his mind and came round to Edmands' view. Ranganathan was never happy with book numbers founded on alphabetical principles. (His basis we shall deal with later.) No one listened to his criticisms because he was attacking an accepted standard.

Cutter was later to take Edmands' method to the highly developed system of author numbers by which he is now pre-eminently known, even though his patrimony rests in other areas (e.g., descriptive cataloging, and the basis of the Library of Congress Classification). Alpha-numeric book number notation had come to stay with Cutter's improvements.

During an annual conference of the American Library Association held on September 25, 1885, another discussion on book numbers was held. There W.I. Fletcher (1844-1917), then Librarian of Amherst College, asked of Cutter whether the combination of letters and numbers led to trouble. Cutter was unequivocal and confident as he said "the combination of letters and numbers leads to just the opposite result. The mind does not easily grasp more than 4 or 5 letters of figures...B29F44 is more easily read than BVDGMO or 129744".[8] Dewey also endorsed Edmand's method of using the initial letter of the author and then translating the early part of the rest of the name into numbers as "the best plan I can conceive for alphabetical arrangement and I hope some one will make the necessary table for applying it".[9] This "some one" was to be Charles Ammi Cutter (1837-1903), and soon after the symposium Cutter was the first to devise a table for author numbers and to sell it commercially. It was the first (1880) of the long line of cutter author number tables. In fact, in 1879 Cutter had cataloged the Winchester Town Library along the lines of his idea. This author table is now lost to us. Comaromi, however, surmised that it was probably composed (as was the third Cutter two-figure table) of three pieces of paste board held together by cloth tape.[10] The 1888 version is available to us. Any word beginning with a consonant (except S) required one letter and two numbers. Two letters were required for a word beginning with a vowel or S, followed by one digit. Three letters were required for the name beginning with Sc. An extract from the table follows:

Ger	31	Have	Ac	1	Ar	Sa	1	Sh
Gerr	32	Hax	Aid	2	Arc	Sai	2	Shao
Ges	33	Hayf	Aig	3	Are	Sal	3	she

Here are a few illustrations of the use of the table:

Beard	B34	Abbot	Ab2
Holmes	H73	Anee	An7
Huxley	H98	Smith	Sm51
		Schopenhaur	Sch6

Cutter explained the mechanism of assigning the decimal notation in a small pamphlet.[11] Later this table was included in the sixth expansion of his Expansive Classification of 1893. Dewey used Cutter's author table in conjunction with his Decimal Classification in 1882 while classifying the collection of the Wellesley College library. As Dewey's personality and position was commanding, his approval of any idea imparted to it a force and fillip that made it succeed. By 1885 the Cutter table was quite popular and librarians swore to its efficacy in arranging their collections. Many enterprising and innovating librarians put these book numbers to many ingenious uses, some of them even useful.[12]

By the mid 1880s cuttering had become a standard practice in US libraries, and the term "cutter number" became synonymous with author number, and even book number. Now "cuttering" is an accepted word in the English language.

Cutter's two-figure table was suitable for small libraries; it "was found inadequate for the large classes of fiction and individual biography" according to Bertha Barden.[13] To meet the need of large and then rapidly expanding libraries, Cutter decided to expand his table to three figures and more names. In 1892 the revision was assigned to Cutter's former assistant, Kate Emery Sanborn (later Mrs. Gardner Jones). Sanborn was then working as a cataloger at the Mercantile Library of St. Louis. Cutter was not able to supervise her work over the great distance that was then a part of life. The result was virtually an independent work that improved considerably upon Cutter's somewhat defective organization.

Sanborn devised a table in which every name irrespective of names beginning with a vowel or S began uniformly with a single letter. It was a welcome change. A and S were followed by three digits that functioned in the same way as decimal fractions, and E, I, O, and U by two digits that behaved like decimal fractions. Sanborn's "expansion" (it was actually a different work, one so radically different from Cutter's two-figure numbers that the two-figure numbers had to be discarded when Sanborn's three-figure table was accepted) appeared in two parts. The first part was for vowels and S. It was published in 1892 and sold by Cutter: *Cutter's Alfabetic-order Table: Alternatives for the Vowels and S* by Miss Kate E. Sanborn. Boston: Library Bureau, 1892. 4 pp. of tables. 33x17 cm. The table for the remaining consonants was published in 1895: *C.A. Cutter's Alfabetic-order Table: Consonants, except S; Altered and Fitted with Three Figures* by Miss Kate E. Sanborn. Boston: Library

Bureau, 1895. 14 p. 33x28 cm. Shortly thereafter the two tables were combined: *C.A. Cutter's Alfabetic-order Table: Consonants except S, and Vowels and S; Altered and Fitted with Three* Figures by Miss Kate E. Sanborn. Boston: Library Bureau, 1896. 18 pp. 33x15 cm.

Sanborn uniformly used one letter followed by from one to three digits, depending upon the letter. Two digits follow vowels (except A) and consonants J, K, Y, and Z. One digit follows Q and X. The rest of the consonants and A are followed by three digits. The table contained approximately 12,000 numbers. To illustrate:

Winston Churchill	C563
Jonathan Ewards	E36
Marcus Quintilian	Q7

Since these numbers behave like decimal fractions, they can be expanded or reduced at will without disturbing neighbouring numbers so long as they have not been used for other authors or subjects. In a small library these numbers can be reduced to one-digit numbers, and can be expanded to even four - or five-digit numbers wherever the collection demands. Henry E. Bliss and Zaidee Brown proposed some simplifying methods.[14-16]

A maor difficulty in the use of Sanborn's "expansion" was that it could not be used to expand the earlier two-figure numbers of the first Cutter author table, even though Cutter's name was in the title. Difficulty or no a three-fgure table was badly needed, and as Cutter was not to publish his own official three-figure table that would be consonant with his two-figure one until five years later, Sanborn's three-figures carried the day, and the next century. Before proceeding further with the story, let us illustrate how different the author tables were (Cutter's two-figure and Sanborn's three-figure):

Author	Cutter Two-figure	Sanborn Three-figure
Matthew Arnold	Ar6	A757
Richard Kimball	K56	K49
Sinclair Lewis	L58	L676
Somerset Maugham	M44	M449
Walter Scott	Sco8	S431
George Bernard Shaw	Sh2	S534
Anthony Quinn	Q4	Q7
Xavier University	X1	X3
Ulrich Zwingli	Z9	Z98

One can appreciate that Cutter was not at all happy with the revision. He was, in fact, quite irritated, especially as the revision was proving to be superior to his and librarians were discarding his two-figure table for her three-figure one. Cutter not only disliked the new work, he also wished to force it from the field. He tried to discredit Sanborn by describing the publication of her work as a "mistake" on his part. In a letter to a journal he candidly wrote that "through some misunderstanding the new ones [tables] were made without any reference to their predecessors, so that the two cannot be used together. I could not ask a volunteer to do her work over again, and so I printed them."[17] In a sour mood Cutter revised his table to three figures and offered it for sale in 1901. In both his old and new tables the first two figures are the same. Lehnus wrote that "Cutter tried to have his new table replace that of Sanborn, but without any effect."[18] The reasons are not difficult to find, of course, though they were hidden from the injured ego of Cutter. The Cutter-Sanborn table is easy to use and in a uniform style. It has also its scientific merit as the allocation of digits to letters comes more closely than that of Cutter to their actual frequency of occurrence as the initial letter of surnames.[19] Moreover, the Cutter-Sanborn table had already become an established practice before Cutter's three-figure table was made available. It is ironic that the Cutter-Sanborn table, a work that Cutter described as a "mistake", is the major living and applied work associated with his name.

In 1969 Esther M. Swift with the assistance of Paul K. Swanson reorganized the Cutter two-and three-figure table and the Cutter-Sanborn three-figure table. The tables, published and distributed first by the H.R. Huntting Company, are now distributed by Libraries Unlimited, Inc. (P.O. Box 3988, Englewood, Colorado, 80155) for the present owner Richard Anmi Cutter, a grandson of Cutter. The tables have been entirely reset as all the letters have been placed in A-Z order, thus making it much easier to use than the older tables that hopscotched through the alphabet. Nor is one column of numbers shared by two columns of letters. Printing errors have been corrected, the physical format upgraded. Until the Swanson-Swift revisions appeared in 1969 libraries had to make do with typed, disfigured, and worn out copies of the tables.[20-22]

There are innumerable adaptations and reprints of the Cutter tables. In many cases necessity drove the adapters to publish their work because the orignal tables or their authorized revisions are still not available everywhere. One such redoing of the Cutter-Sanborn table on card thick stock in mineograph form has been made available in India (1972) as a "revised edition." Its introduction was specially rewritten to illustrate use of the table with Indian names. It is published and distributed by the Indian Bibliographical Centre, College Road, Ludhiana, Punjab, India.[23] Another Indian Cutter-Sanborn reprint has been made available on thick card stock with improved printing, but no preface or introduction.[24] On the pattern of the cutter tables many other tables for other scripts have been locally divised.

But let us return to the development of other book number systems. In 1881 A.P. Massey of the Case Library in Cleveland proposed a method of arranging biography and literature. He suggested literal mnemonics, such as B for biography and F for fiction.[25] The class number was subdivided by numbers standing for authors' names. These digits, though preceded by a dot, were not decimal fractions. The system did not catch the fancy of many librarians; it was consigned to the dustbin of history. Too bad, in a way, for his distribution of numbers to names was one of the best ever allotted. Massey's table has been described in some detail by John Comaromi, and evaluated for its alphabetical distribution by Don Lehnus.[26-27] Before we leave Massey, let us show you his number for *Quentin Durward* by Sir Walter Scott:

F
746
14

F stood for fiction, 746 for Scott in Massey's distribution of A-Z over the integers 1-999, and 14 for the fourteenth piece of fiction by Scott. If any integer was used up before an author arrived too late, a decimal fraction was added to the integer without benefit of decimal point or clergy. That is,

F
746
301

would be for the first work by someone named Scott who wrote a piece of fiction acquired after Sir Walter had been established and after the next Scott number (747) had been assigned to Xavier Scott. It was an awkward system, but the allotment of integers to letters was probably the best ever devised. Only Schwartz's second scheme rivals it.

In 1885 a new line in book numbers was intorduced to the world, one based not on author's name but upon the year of publication. In that year Walter Stanley Biscoe (1853-1933), a trusted lieutenant of Melvil Dewey, a major figure in the development of the DDC and at that time with Dewey at Columbia College in New York City, published his concept of the chronological book number.[28] Since that time such book numbers have become a legitimate alternative to book numbers based upon the name of the author. It was in certain areas a welcome alternative to alphabetical arrangement, even though the alphanumeric notation betrays one into thinking that the arrangement is alphabetical. Upon Biscoe we must bestow the honor of having been the father of chronological book numbers. Though the antecedents of the Biscoe table are easily discernible in Dewey's accession method, Biscoe "credited Cutter, Edmands, and Schwartz for the basic idea of his time table."[29] (We must admit that it boggles the mind to imagine how *three* people can be the source of *one* idea. but, then, the calculus of intellectual discovery or invention probably requires a range of inputs for one output. Perhaps the credit was for the overall idea of book numbers than for his table specifically, for there is no doubt that Schwartz, Edmands, and Cutter are the great names in the evolution of book numbers.)

An extract from the Biscoe time table follows:

A	BC era	G	1800-1809	V	1950-1959
B	AD 1-999	H	1810-1819	.....	
C	1000-1499	I	1820-1829	Y	1980-1989
D	1500-1599	....			
E	1600-1699				
F	1700-1799	N	1870-1879	Z	1990-1999

The table was cleverly devised to be based on literary warrant, as modern books (published from the 19th century onwards—a large majority of books in any library) are denoted by two digits only.

For example:

1958 V8
1987 Y7

Clever or not, one wonders whether Biscoe thought the world would end at 2000, a scant full generation after his death. Well, his world was gloomy when he closed his eyes on it.

The table was applied to the science collection of Columbia College on an experimental basis, chronological arrangement seeming to be best in the scientific and technical areas. Dewey approved of the system (how could he not; he was the Librarian of Columbia College), and did what he could to promote it, going so far as to recommend it in the second edition of the DDC. (A little known fact is that Biscoe was the primary editor of the epochal second edition.) Therein Dewey wrote:

> Its advantage is in presenting the historical development of the subject, the books written earliest being on the left, the latest work on the right, and then of any given book it is evident that all those on the left were written before it, all those on the right after it. In science this has special value...A translation system of dates makes the numbering system of the year more compact and satisfactory.[30]

On the other hand, Dewey was apt in pointing out that chronological subarrangement should be used only in open access libraries. In closed-access libraries the readers do not have the advantage of browsing through the collection; consequently, a chronological arrangement will find no utility. The situation would be analogous to that of a fine flower wasting its fragrance upon the desert air, and its beauty to absent eyes. Moreover, a chronological arrangement is more a tool of display than of retrieval. In closed-access libraries, alphabetical arrangement (comparatively a better retrieval device) is preferable. Biscoe's system is also silent upon the many complications of sub-arrangement. Ranganathan would later take the idea to a highly developed system, which the reader will come to later in this work.

In 1893 C.R. Olin, Librarian of Buchtel College (later the University of Akron) devised a table for collective biography, based on Cutter's two-figure author table.[31] According to his table, collective biography arranged by the editor or compiler preceded the individual biographies arranged by the name of the biographee (the subject). He used the latter A followed by the numbers 11-99 to represent all names A to Z of compilers and editors of collective biographies.[32] To avoid confusion all the biographies beginning with A were denoted by two letters, the rest of the names of individual biographies by Cutter's two-figure author table. The author's initial was used as a work mark to distinguish two or more biographies of the same person by different authors.

L. Stanley Jast (1868-1944) of the United Kingdom devised in 1912 a scheme of alphabetical author marks.[33] It shows that the British should avoid original thought in this regard, and is based on the primitively simple practice of using only the first two letters of the author's surname for alphabetical arrangement by author. In those cases where there were more than one author—as there would be many such cases—having the same first two letters in their surnames, then would they be differentiated by adding 1, 2, or 3 and so on to their first two initial letters of the surname for the last author marks.[34] For example:

Williams	Wi
Wilfred	Wil
Wilson	Wi2
Wiston	Wi3

Obviously, the resulting arrangement will not be strictly alphabetical, as 1, 2, and so on are to be added to the author's name as they are accessioned in the library, and not according to the dictionary sequence. It is a very simple combination of using the initial of the author's surname combined with the accession method. This same principle is followed in distinguishing more than one work by an author on the same subject. This method has no better status than that of a locally devised method that should not be allowed to travel from home.

William S. Merrill (1866-1969) devised in 1912 an alphabetical table of 99 numbers (denoted by 01-99).[35] Merrill's table can be found on pages 27-28 of James Duff Brown's Subject Classification (2nd edition, 1914), and in a few of the earlier textbooks on classification. An extract from his table is given below to give the reader an idea of his sparsely numbered author table:

01	A	13	Bum
02	Agre	14	C
03	Ali	15	Carr
04	Ap	16	Cha
06	B	46	K
07	Ban	47	L
08	Bax	48	Lang
09	Bend	49	Law
10	Beno	96	Wats
11	Bon	97	Wha
12	Brin	98	Wit
		99	X-Z

Obviously, the resulting arrangement will be a crude approximation of alphabetical order. The notation, however, is pure, being of Indo-arabic integers only. The initial letter of the author's surname is ignored. Consequently, confusion would result if the system was used with the DDC. By no means does it show any advantage over Cutter's table. The thoughtful would expect that such a system would be used only in desperation, and they would be correct; it registered a retrograde step in the history of book numbers. No where is it written that things must get better; often they do not.

Cutter's Expansive Classification provided the basis for the outline of the Library of Congress Classification that first saw the light of day in 1898. The complete Classification was published in fascicles up to 1940, though several editions of several segments appeared during that period. It was, of course, a colossal undertaking, one as much admired for the attempt as for the result. The first fasciule to be published was that for library science and bibliography (Z), a reasonable place to begin-organizing thought on recorded thought. For book numbers the Cutter-Sanborn table was adopted for both subject and author numbers. For fiction, however, the Library turned to the Cutter three-figure table, probably because it possessed almost twice as many numbers as its rival the Cutter-Sanborn table. It was a mistake to do so, but not so great a mistake as having a PZ (fiction) table at all-which much later was largely rectified by moving fiction to the national literatures and to the authors therein. (But, then, time has shown that the minds at the Library of Congress have never been graced with a towering intelligence.) However, no table was followed strictly, according to Anna C. Laws, who worked at the Library at that time and who wrote the first book on LC author notation.[36] As the Library of Congress Classification (LCC) is a close classification-one of the very closest, book numbers are broad and usually consist of an initial alphabet and one or two digits that behave like decimal fractions. The number of digits, however, varies from class to class as literary warrant varies from class to class.[37] Apart from the work by Anna C. Laws there are now several sources on the book numbering practice of the Library of Congress, e.g., by Comaromi[38] and by Immroth[39] and that found in various issues of the Library of Congress's Cataloging Service Bulletin.

In many cases, the book number is an integral part of the LCC number. Though different segments of the Classification follow somewhat different shelflisting procedures, normally one or two (and in rare cases five) digits are added to the initial of the author's name from a standard table that follows:

(1) After the initial letter S, for the second letter of the author's surname use the number as indicated:

a	ch	e	h-i	m-p	t	u
2	3	4	5	6	7-8	9

For example, Smith would be assigned .S6 (the point to show that the number is to behave like a decimal fraction).

(2) After the initial letter in Qu, for the third letter use the given digit:

a	c	e	o	r	y
e	4	5	6	7	9

For example, Queen would be assigned .Q5, Qureshi .Q7.

(3) After any other initial consonant, for the second letter of the author's surname use the given digit:

a	e	i	o	r	u	y
3	4	5	6	7	8	9

For example, Robert .R6, Putnam .P8, Carter .C3, Corbett .C6.

(4) After initial voles for the second letter in the name use following digits:

b-d	e-m	n	p	r	s-t
23	4	5	6	7	8

For example, Adams .A3, Archer .A7.

All these variations and the staff manual for assigning book numbers have been published in a variety of publications. These alphabetical marks, it should be noted, are also used to indicate subjects as well as authors. What can be put in alphabetical order can be coded by the LC book number system. How well the LC book numbers agree with the alphabetical assortment that it organizes has not been established. One of us (Comaromi) concluded years ago that the LC distribution was badly canted. But a leviathan's course is difficult to alter, so he said nothing regarding the bias. By virtue of LC's card services, its MARC record, and its Cataloging-in-Publication, LC class numbers and its book numbers are widely used all over the world.

A British librarian, James Duff Brown (1862-1914), devised in 1906 two book numbering methods, one alphabetical and the other chronological; he included both in his Subject Classification.[40] His "Extended Date Table" subarranged books by their publication year. The range of the table extended from 1450 to 2125- i.e., 126 years more than Biscoe's table devised for the same purpose. (Duff's mind was obviously more expansive than those of his professional contemporaries.) Within the span every year is denoted by two lowercase Roman letters. The outline of his table is as follows:

1450-1475	aa-az
1476-1501	ba-bz
...	
1840-1865	pa-pz
1866-1891	qa-qz
...	
2100-2125	za-zz

To illustrate:

1450	aa	1900	ri
1451	ab	1902	rk
1452	ac	1904	rm
1700	jq	1918	sa
1701	jr	1919	sb
1702	js	1920	sc

The notation is pure, simple, and easy to write if one knows the lowercase Roman alphabet. However, the table was not built on a proportionate allocation of notation: the less used years of the 15th to 18th centuries are denoted by two letters as are the heavily used years of the twentieth century. Secondly, though built on a regular structure, the table is not mnemonic; one has to refer to it every time to assign a number. It was no advancement over Biscoe's method.

An author table to suit Indian names was devised in 1916 by the American librarian Asa Don Dickinson (1876-1960), then on a short term assignment in India as librarian of the Punjab University in Lahore. Dickinson is credited correctly with the honor of having introduced the DDC into India. He devised his author table as a part of his book the *Punjab Library Primer* (1916) a pioneering work on library science in India.[41] The book number system is claimed to be followed still in some Indian libraries.[42] Though Dickinson's work is now unavailable, his book number method has been explained in Hindi in a work by M. Zuber and S. P. Agrawal.[43] This is a simplified Indian adaptation of the Cutter-Sanborn table. In the table each author number is comprised of a letter followed by two digits (that behave like decimal fractions). X, Y, and Z are followed by one digit. To illustrate:

Adams	A22
Bell	B42
Eddington	E27
Shakespeare	S32
Xavier	X3
Young	Y7

For his Colon Classification (1933) S.R. Ranganathan (1892-1972) devised a system of book numbers no less systematic or detailed than his Classification. His book number system is a complete system in itself, and like his Classification is fully faceted in structure. It has been included and explained in every edition of the Colon Classification.[44] It is an integral part of his Classification; it complements CC numbers. Such an important role for book numbers was ensured by his canon of book numbers enunciated in the *Prolegomena*.[45] Despite its close association with the Colon Classification number, his book numbers can be applied profitably with any classification system.[46]

The formula for a CC book number is:

[L] [F] [Y] [A] . [V] - [S] ; [C] :y [EVN]

Language, form, and year of publication are the three major characteristics taken into consideration. The formula also provides to keep together the host and its associated works in the form of supplements, copies, commentaries, and subcommentaries. The year facet remains the linch pin of his book numbers. All other facets are secondary, nor necessarily present. Though complex in its entirety, it remains the only scientific and complete system of chronological book numbers. Ranganathan's debt to Biscoe is obvious, but he transformed Biscoe's simple device into a complete system. The nucleus remains the same, but the superstructure is that of Ranganathan.

In 1961 Fremont Rider (1885-1962) proposed another chronological book number method as a part of his International Classification.[47] Rider devised no new date table; basically, he set down another Biscoe time table. Rider's book numbers arrange works by the decade of publication-one letter denotes a decade. Instead of individualizing the works down to a year, the decades are further subdivided by author. Thus it comes to be a curious mixture of Chronological and alphabetical arrangement. The Rider book number consists of two Roman capital letters, the first standing for the decade of publicaton as taken from the Biscoe table, and the second for the initial letter of the author's surname. Obviously, the two letters may not completely individualize the document as two or more authors with the same initial letter in their surnames may happen to write on the same subject in a given decade. In such cases, the two digits are further individualized by adding 1, 2, 3, etc. to the book number. This system, which may be called a chronological-alphabetical system, does not seem to possess any edge over a purely aphabetical or chronological system. A decade is too long a span of time in the book publication of thought to be taken as an unfragmented unit for arrangement. Subarrangement will, *de facto*, be an alphabetical one.

Cutter tables, being based upon American names (or at least upon names of authors whose works are acquired in American libraries), are inevitably not so efficacious for the ethnic names that crop up in other countries that do not feed the population growth of the United States. By showing how Cutter tables are utterly unable to differentiate among many Indian names, the National Library of India at Calcutta has shown that the Cutter table has to be expanded to an unwieldy six or seven digits.[48] Of course, a half a brain would tell anyone that the Indians need their own Cutter numbers. But, then, the other half of the brain says that we are soon to come to planetary Cutter numbers. (There has to be, somewhere, a Cutter table that can accommodate all alphabets.) To obviate some of the difficulties of an alphabet that does not fit, many locally devised tables for native names have come into existence. One such table table was devised and published in 1961 by the National Library of India-a depository of the Indian Publications Copyright Act. The table was designed on the literary warrant of many Indian names of varying linguistic, regional, and ethnic groups. The table is able to differentiate authors with the same surname, but different forenames. Many gaps have been left for further expansion. The table is complicated in that given the same initial, some names begin with the same two letters:

Bapu	B628	Sadasivan, K.	S152
Bhajan	Bh236	Sekhron, P.	Se321

And for some letters (Namely, O, Q, W, X, and Z) two digits follow the initial (single) letter. For the rest the number of digits is three. Indian names have been trasliterated into the Roman script by the Hunterian system, and original forms of the Anglicized Indian names have been used:

Vasu	for	Bose
Thakur	for	Tagore

Corporate and geographic names have not been included. If any other library is using the system, it is not known by us.

Another author table for the English alphabet was devised by the Indian Librarian Gopi Chand Makkar (b.1944) in 1974. It is known as the three-number author table, because for every name three digits are used preceded by the initial letter of the surname.[49] The table (claimed to be "refreshingly original in concept") is said to be prepared without any bias to any racial, ethnic, or national names. In fact, it has been prepared in blissful ignorance of the mechanism of an author table, prepared merely by the permuted combination of four letters taken one at a time and by uniformly allocating three decimal digits to every set of four letters. In the table number allotment for the letter A and its various combinations, one can substitute any other corresponding letter. It means, say, that Ains, Bins, Dins, Kins, Lins, and Zins all have the same three-digit number that is distinguished only by the initial letter of the author's surname. Every number uniformly begins with the two initial letters of the surname:

Ains	Ai562	Aam	Aa511
Bins	Bi562	Ram	Ra511
Dins	Di562	Sam	Sa511

Thus each alphabet yields 18,280 numbers, and the whole table can yield 475,280 numbers, though most of them will be constructed of impossible combinations and unprintable words. In the printed table only the group of words beginning with A have been given, as an illustration and guide. By such a practice the scheme becomes symmetrical in structure. It also makes provision for bringing together different volumes, editions, and copies of the same work. The author has enumerated some twelve points of dubious superiority over the Cutter tables. Dubious because it is futile to try to assimilate good from both the worlds of Cutter and Ranganathan, for if all the attributes are taken together, the book number becomes a rather involved and unnecessarily complicated string of alphabets and numbers.

After Ranganathan no notable strides have been made in the development of book numbers. No new system has come to the fore and nothing seems in the offing. Book numbers figured in the library literature in the sprouting years of this now waning century. But discussions in the periodical literature gradually ceased by the 1920's. The significant place that once was given to the study and description of book numbers in every standard textbook on cataloguing and classification has gradually declined. W.C.B.

Sayers (1881-1960) made a considerably detailed study of book numbers and allocated to it a respectable place in every edition of his justly famous classification manual. Still, the reviser of the manual, Arthur Maltby, made only a passing reference to book numbers as if they were no more than pepper gound upon the salad. Many new works on classification have barely touched upon book numbers. To the current generation book numbers are as valuable as boxes to hold ice. Classification conferences eschew discussion of book numbers; it seems librarians collude to defy a fine organization of classes.

Despite such negligence, there are books on the subject of book numbers by those who whistle into the wind and who believe that mind is transcendent no matter what convenience thinks.

The first book on book numbers appeared in 1917; it was devoted only to LC practice. The theory and practice of book numbers was ably set forth by Bertha Barden in 1937. Her manual is for students and practitioners alike; it gives rules for the use of book numbers with any scheme. The next work after a long pause came in 1980; it is a stimulating study of book numbers by the late Donald J. Lehnus (1934-1983). In his book, the history of book numbers has been fully related, and Lehnus went on to give many useful details in the application of them. Closely upon the publication of Lehnus's book came a similar bok by John P. Comaromi (1937-1991): *Book Numbers,* that treated the history of book numbers less fully than Lehnus, treated the use of Cutter-Sanborn numbers about the same, but went on to explicate Library of Congress book numbering practice in details. Both are standard works, but regretfully neither attracted many reviews or created a stir in the readers for whom they were intended. Such reviewer silence confirms the lack of interest in a topic that provides a fundamental organization of the classes of a library classification. And both books ignored Ranganathan's book number system. This vacuum however, has now been filled.[50-51]

This brief chronicle cannot hope to be complete; it is rather a descriptive catalog of major book number systems. Home-made systems rival the number of stars visible on a moonlit night. The literature is far in arrears in reporting the methods tried. A sort of literature deflation is at work; the theory of book numbers shrinks to nothing, and minds do not deign to address themselves to the problem of organizing classes. In many classification systems, and consequently in libraries, book numbers are given scant attention, less even than a step mother would give to another woman's children (as Comaromi suggested).[52] Many classification theorists are silent on the issue; it is yet another reason for the hodgepodge methods that pass for book numbers. For all the above reasons, and probably for a few more, no formal history of book numbers can be traced in its entirety; yet without the history of book numbers, the history of library classification cannot be told completely (as Dr. I. Dahlberg confided in a persnal discussion with one of us).

References

1. Comaromi, John P. *The Eighteen Editions of the Dewey Decimal Classification*. Albany, N.Y.: Forest press, 1976; p. 99
2. Dewey, Melvil. "Eclectic Book-numbers", *Library Journal* 11 Aug.-Sept. 186): 296-301 (*quoted* in Lehnus, Donald J. *Book Numbers*. Chicago: ALA, 1980; p. 26)
3. Barden, Bertha R. *Book Numbers: a Manual for Students with a Basic Code of Rules*. Chicago: ALA, 1937; pp. 5-6
4. Schwartz, Jacob. "A New Classification and Notation", *Library Journal* 7 (July-Aug. 1882): 148-166
5. Lehnus, Donald J. *Book Numbers*. p. 53
6. Comaromi, John P *Op. cit*. p. 100
7. "Plans for Numbering, with Especial Reference to Fiction," *Library Journal* 4 (Feb. 1879): 38-47
8. "Cutter Author-numbers in Connection with the Dewey Decimal Classification," *Library Journal* 13 (Sept.-Oct. 1888): 308-309 (*quoted in* Lehnus, p. 35)
9. "Plans for numbering..." *Op. cit*. p. 47
10. Comaromi, John P. *Book Numbers*. p. 40
11. Cutter, C.A. *How to get Books with an Explanation of the New Way of Marking Books*. Boston: Press of Rockwell and Churchill, 1882; pp. 14-15
12. Swan, Charles H. "Alfab-order Table for Names of Places," *Library Journal* 11 (April 1886): 118
13. Barden, Bertha R. *Book Numbers*. p. 7
14. Bliss, Henry E. "Simplified Book Notation," *Library Journal* 35 (1910): 545
15. Bliss, Henry E. "A Simplified Alphabetic Order Table," *Library Journal* 37 (1912): 71-72
16. Brown, Zaidee. "More about Cutter Numbers," *Library Journal* 57 (1932): 437
17. Cutter, C.A. Letter to the Editor, *Public Libraries* 5 (June 1900): 243 (*quoted in* Lehnus, pp. 39-40)
18. Lehnus, p. 41
19. Lehnus, p. 63
20. *Cutter-Sanborn Three-figure Author Table*. Swanson-Swift revision. Chicopee, Mass.: H.R. Huntting, 1969; 33 pp. of tables

21. *C.A. Cutter's Three-figure Author Table*. Swanson-Swift revision. Chicopee, Mass.: H.R. Huntting, 1969; 29 pp. of tables
22. *C.A. Cutter's Two-figure Author Table*. Swanson-Swift revision. Chicopee, Mass.: H.R. Huntting, 1969; 4 pp. of tables.
23. *Cutter-Sanborn Three-figure Author Table*. Rev. ed. Ludhiana: Indian Bibliographical Centre, 1972; 40 p.
24. *C.A. Cutter's Three-figure Alfabetic order Table*. Fully rev. ed. Jammu: Light and Life Publishers, 1972. 26 p.
25. Massey, A.P. "Classification of Fiction," *Library Journal* 6 (Jan. 1881): 7-9
26. Comaromi, John P. *Book Numbers*, pp. 41-42
27. Lehnus, p. 23
28. Biscoe, Walter Stanley. "Chronological Arrangement on Shelves," *Library Journal* 10 (Sept.-Oct. 1885): 245-246
29. Lehnus, p. 23
30. *Dewey, Melvil, Decimal Classification and Relativ Index*. 2nd ed. Boston: Library Bureau, 1885; p. 37 (*quoted in* Lehnus, p. 25)
31. Olin, C.R. "An Author Table for Collective Biography," *Library Journal* 18 (May 1893): 144
32. Lehnus, p. 24
33. Jast, L. Stanley. "Book Numbers," *Library World* 3 (1912): 120-123, 150-152
34. Phillips, W. Howard. *A Primer of Book Classification*. Rev. ed. London: Association of Assistant Librarians, 1951; p. 54
35. Merrill, William Stetson. "Merrill Book Numbers," *Public Libraries* 17 (1912): 127-129
36. Laws, Anna C. *Author Notation in the Library of Congress*. Washington: GPO, 1917; pp. 5-6
37. Lehnus, p. 43
38. Comaromi, John P. *Book Numbers*, p. 92-122
39. Immroth, John P. *A Guide to Library of Congress Classification*. 2nd ed. Littleton, Colo.: Libraries Unlimited, 1971; p. 48
40. Brown, James Duff. Subject Classification. 3rd ed. Rev. by J.D. Stewart. London: Grafton, 1939; secs. 32-27, pp. 27-32
41. Dickinson, Asa Don. *Punjab Library Primer*. Lahore: University of Punjab, 1916; 242 p. and Anwar, Mumtaz Ali "Asa Don Dickinsn", *Third World Lib*. 1(2) Winter 1990-91: 7-15
42. Saxena, T.P. Foreword to *Three-number Author Tables*, by G.C. Makkar. New Delhi: Today and Tomorrow's Printers and Publishers, 1974; p. xi
43. Zuber, Mohammed and Agrawal, S.P. *Pustak-Sankhya Preveshika*. [Introduction to book numbers]. Aligarh: Shanker Prakashan, 1954; pp. 24-52
44. Ranganathan, S.R. *Colon Classification*. 6th ed. Bombay: Asia Publishing House, 1959. Chapt. 03, pp. 109-117
45. Ranganathan, S.R. *Prolegomena to Library Classification*. 3rd ed., assisted by M.A. Gopinath. Bombay: Asia Publishing House, 1967. Sec. UB2 (p. 503)
46. Satija, M.P. *Manual of Practical Colon Classification*. New Delhi: Sterling, 1984; p. 95
47. Rider, Fremont A. *Rider's International Classification for the Arrangement of Books on the Shelves of General Libraries*. Middleton, Conn.: the Author, 1961. Introduction
48. India. National Library. *Author Table for Indian Names*. Calcutta: The Library, 1961; viii, 255p.

49. Makkar, G.C. *Three number Author Table*. New Delhi: Today and Tomorrow's Printers and Publishers, 1974; xiv, 118p.
50. Satija, M.P. *A Primer on Ranganathan's Book Numbers*. Delhi: Mittal Publications, 1987; xvii, 87 p. ISBN 81-7099-004-1
51. Satija, M.P. and Agrawal, S.P.: *Book Numbers: Some Indian Methods*. New Delhi: Concept, 1990; 96p ISBN 81-7022-238-9
52. Comaromi, John P. *Book Numbers*. p. 5

CHAPTER 4

Chronological Book Numbers: Pros and Cons

If the year of publication is made the basis of subarranging the items that fall in a class, then the resulting book number may be called a *chronological book number*. The year of publication can be coded or written as such; or, some other method, say, use of the accession number, may be used to serve as a chronological book number. It is not necessary that the year of publication be the only and the first attribute to serve as the chronological book number. (For example, in the Colon Classification a book number has as a maximum eight facets in the formula, the first being the language of the document.)

Cutter numbers (author arrangement) and the chronoloical system of book numbers are of equal age, and have come down to us simultaneously. Librarians choose between the two methods (whether they know it or not); some libraries have even employed both systems to arrange their books. For example, Cutter used both methods for subarranging the science collection of his library.

One system may suit a library better than the other. Anna C. Laws long ago affirmed that the chronological method of arranging books can be used profitably in scholarly libraries.[1]

Arguments that favour the chronological system follow:

(1) Chronological book numbers have simple, straightforward tables. The mnemonic quality that attaches to them is great. Once they are used they need be consulted infrequently. Author numbers, on the other hand, belong to a complicated family of numbers suited to names, and many family members cannot remember the name of each member, and are embarrassed when memory fails at an inopportune time. It is not only necessary to refer to the author table every time to assign a book number, it also takes more time. Hence, chronological arrange-

ment satisfies the Ranganathan's Fourth Law: Save the time of the staff.

(2) There is a chronological number for every year, but there cannot be a Cutter number for every name.

(3) In the case of author numbers, there may not be any certainty that the Cutter number always means the translation of the author's name. Sometimes it means the first word of the title in the case of a title main entry, or the name of a corporate body in the case of an institution being taken as the author. It may mean the subject in the case of a biography, as biographies are arranged by their subject, not by the person who writes about a person (in order to bring all biographies of a person together). But a year number means a year number.

(4) S.R. Ranganathan was of the opinion that since the year of publication can be known from the book number, so it need not be repeated in descriptive cataloging—in this way simplifying cataloging somewhat. (Whoa, says the reader; Ranganathan obviously never met many descriptive catalogers, nor understood the value of an imprint. Nevertheless, that is what he said and believed.)

(5) The same author may get different Cutter numbers in different classes. Thus, such a system is not an absolute system that is true here, there, and everywhere. It is un-mnemonic, and a source of confusion.

(6) Arrangement by author violates Ranganathan's Canon of Impartiality: if there are more than two authors, the book will get a Cutter number for the major author only, and be arranged accordingly. Lesser, and not so lesser, authors will feel ignored, and justly so. The Canon of Impartiality ensures equal credit to however many writers produced a work. In chronological numbers no such problem invades fairness.

(7) A chronological sequence fulfills the demands of the Canon of Helpful Sequence. Ranganathan considered a chronological sequence of books in a class to be more helpful than any other to most readers. Readers usually wish to get the latest material, or the oldest, or that pertaining to a specific span of time, accordingly they may get their material at one place—and in one lot on the shelf. Chronological arrangement, therefore, satisfies the fourth law of library science: Save the time of the reader.

(8) A chronological subarrangement helps to trace the develop-

ment of a subject over a given period. The method, therefore, may also be helpful in writing trend reports, state-of-the-art reports, and the history of a given subject. In a library using such a method the browsing of books will be more rewarding.

(9) The chronological method can be helpful in weeding out obsolete books prior to a certain fixed date.

(10) Cutter numbers are for the Roman alphabet and primarily for American names and names derived from part of Europe. This means that Cutter number tables have to be prepared not only for every other alphabet and script, but also for many different linguistic, ethnic, and national groups of persons. This problem does not occur in chronological book numbers.

The superiority of a chronological arrangement over an alphabetical one can be corroborated by evidence from both authorities and self-practice. Melvil Dewey, who appended Biscoe's chronological book number table from the 7th through the 13th edition of the DDC, advocated the use of a chronological system as being one useful in the sciences and in the useful arts.[2] Biscoe, credited to be the father of chronological book numbers, applied his system to the science and technology books of the Columbia College Library (now Columbia University). He claimed that "any one who had used the chronological method swore to its superiority over other means of arranging books".[3] The superiority of chronological book numbers has been attested further by the rising trend of arranging entries in a bibliography by the years of their publication. The Harvard system of citing references is predominantly chronological, as after the author the year of publication of a document is enclosed within parentheses.[4]

To number the disadvantages of chronological book numbers:

(1) Most such system are not fully developed.

(2) It will be of less use to employ chronological book numbers in a closed access library, as there will be no reader to avail himself of the utility of a chronological system. This argument was put forward by Melvil Dewey in 1886.[5]

(3) It has been argued that chronological book numbers are a better tool of organization than of retrieval. In many classes books are better located by the name of the author than by the year of their publication. This may square with the Canon of the Recall Value: an author of a book is more easily remembered

than its year of publication. A most serious disadvantage voiced is that a chronological arrangement separates two books by the same author on the same subject. Worse, it also separates different editions of the same work, unless some device is formed to bring them together. T.P. Saxena in his foreword to an author table argues that in the days of open access, chronological arrangement "has not found favour with the reader" for the above two reasons.[6] Chronological systems have, indeed, these two disadvantages, but they are not as serious as posed. His misgivings are not based on experience. As far as the separation of the different editions of the same work is concerned, it is a remediable defect. As far as bringing books together by the same author, this demand is easily met by the author catalog. Yet, inspite of their many advantages, chronological book numbers remain less popular than alphabetical author tables.

References

1. Laws, Anna C. *Author Notation in the Library of Congress.* Washingtn, D.C.: Govt. Printing Office, 1917; pp. 15-17
2. Dewey, Melvil, *Dewey Decimal Classification and Relative Index*, 18th edition, Albany, N.y.: Forest Press, 1979; v1 p. 94
3. Comaromi, John P. *Book Numbers.* Littleton, Colo.: Libraries Unlimited, 1981; p. 46
4. Harrod, L.M.P. *Harrod's Librarians' Glossary.* 7th ed., rev. by Ray Prytherch. Aldershot: Gower, 1990 pp. 282-283
5. Dewey, Melvil, "Eclectic Book Numbers," *Library Journal* 11 (Aug.-Sept. 1886): 296-301
6. Saxena, T.P. Foreword to the *Three Number Author Table* by G.C. Makkar. New Delhi: Today and Tomorrow's Printers and Publishers, 1974; p. xii

CHAPTER 5

Biscoe's Chronological Book Numbers

In the history of librarianship, W.S. Biscoe (1853-1933) will always be remembered as a trusted lieutenant of Melvil Dewey. Son of Thomas Curtis and Ellen Elmore Rider, he was born on the 14th of February 1853, in Grafton, Massachusetts. He obtained his BA from Amherst College in 1874, where he was a classmate of Melvil Dewey. He earned his MA in 1877. In between those years (i.e., during 1875-1876) he served as librarian of the public library at Taunton, Mass. He joined Amherst College, his alma mater, as assistant librarian from 1876-1879; and as acting librarian in 1879, after the departure of Dewey from Amherst to Boston. In 1883, Dewey invited Biscoe to Columbia, where Biscoe remained until 1889 as a cataloger and lecturer in classification at the school of library economy, founded and headed by Dewey. Here Biscoe organized the Columbia College Library under the direction of Dewey. Above all, he remained intimately involved in the preparation of the crucial second edition of the DDC (1885) John Comaromi, historian and later editor of the DDC, wrote: "Biscoe would play a major role in determining the shape of the DDC."[1] Biscoe was at Columbia when he published his chronological book number table in 1885.

Dewey, in fact, had full faith in Biscoe's ability and sincerity. Much of the work of revising and bringing out new editions of the DDC was delegated first to him. Biscoe's devotion to Dewey and his work remains exemplary. In 1889, he followed Dewey to Albany, New York, to work as a cataloging librarian and member of the faculty of the library school Dewey was to establish there. There he remained until 1929, when he retired from the New York State Library. He enthusiastically participated in national and regional library associations, and was elected vice-president of the New

York Library Association for two terms: 1893-1894 and 1901-1902. He died in 1933 before his work was done and before he was ready.

Dewey regarded Biscoe more highly than he ever regarded anyone in librarianship. He wrote of him early in their relationship:

> In all the work from its first publication to the present, the most extended and most valued assistance has come from my college classmate, associate, and friend, Mr. Walter Stanley Biscoe, who was my first assistant in the Amherst College Library, in the charge of which he succeeded me, only resigning to accept again in 1883 the place next to me in the Columbia College Libraries, where he is now Librarian in-charge of Classification and Catalogs. Of the rare unselfishness and loyalty with which he has constantly supported me, giving without compensation time needed for rest and recreation, to advancing work in which he shared my interest, the fitting record is inscribed in this book which best represents his service...[2]

This is, indeed, high praise. Biscoe must have been extremely important to Dewey.

Biscoe, a contemporary of Cutter as well as of Dewey, lived in that hectic period of library history when what molds us today was first formulated and accepted. Biscoe was a classifier of deep experience and, probably, the person most engaged in the development of the second edition of the DDC. He bequeathed to the library world a class a sub-arrangement that would assist users in their intellectual endeavors at the same time as its would organize a collection most productively. He proposed to subarrange books by year of publication. He designed a table to convert the year of publication into a simple alphanumeric notation. The table in extended form is reproduced below:

A 100 BC	H 1810-1819
B 1-999	I 1820-1829
C 1000-1499	J 1830-1839
D 1500-1599	K 1840-1849
E 1600-1699	L 1850-1859
F 1700-1799	M 1860-1869
G 1800-1809	N 1870-1879

O 1880-1889[3]	U 1940-1949
P 1890-1899	V 1950-1959
Q 1900-1909	W 1960-1969
R 1910-1919	X 1970-1979
S 1920-1929	Y 1980-1989
T 1930-1939	Z 1990-1999

The original table as published in 1885 went only up to the letter O1880-1889. Biscoe obviously thought that his device was a temporal one that would one day be superceded by a superior means that the future would reveal.

Claiming many genuine advantages of his system, Biscoe wrote:

> I urge that the chronological order gives additional knowledge, not duplicating information supplied elsewhere by the other catalogs. The accession catalog [accession register] gives the order in which books are received in the library. The author catalog tells what each person has written [and gives the editions of each piece of work]; the chronological arrangement shows us what each person has written; the chronological arrangement shows us what each year has produced on the topic we are investigating. It adds a real value to the shelflist which is no longer arbitrary, but which conveys knowledge peculiarly its own. The shelves are an object lesson constantly before the eyes of every user of the library.[4]

Dewey endorsed Biscoe's view and echoed Biscoe on several occasions. Dewey was a scholar, experimenter, innovator, and an informed critic of book numbers; he did much to promote the Biscoe system: he recommended it to the users of the second edition in 1885, to those of the fourth edition of 1891, and the sixth of 1899. Dewey recommended Biscoe's system along with the Cutter author tables and the Olin table for arranging biographies in the seventh through thirteenth editions. In the fourth edition (1891) Dewey wrote of Biscoe's numbers:

> Time numbers: A second arrangement of books under

> class numbers is chronological by dates of first publication. Its advantage is in presenting the historical development of the subject, the book written earliest being on the left, the latest work on the right, and then of any given book it is evident that all those on the left were written before it, all those on the right after it. In science this has special value, while in literature the author arrangement is better. A translation system of dates devised by W.S. Biscoe makes the numbering of the year more compact and satisfactory than to write the date in full.[5]

Rudiments or weak antecedents of Biscoe's time numbers can be discerned easily in Dewey's accession method. Nevertheless, Biscoe credited others for his thought, specifically Cutter, Edmands, an Schwartz—which at this distance makes eminent sense. Credit to Dewey there was none, but we suspect that Biscoe was honest in his revelation of sources. Whatever the case, his ideal was comparatively bold and fresh. It was then and is now a worthy alternative to alphabetical arrangment.

Biscoe's date table enumerated time periods up to 1889, where they ended at the letter O 1880-1889-the current decade at that time. Later his table was extended to Z, which covered the entire century. Even now, its limited period has become a favorite issue with critics of the system. Cutter wrote:

> Mr. Biscoe's scheme for giving dates briefly is admirable. It has only two defects. First, it is not self-interpreting, it does not suggest its meaning, but has to be understood by a sheer effort of memory. But I do not see how this could be otherwise, if I did I would make a better table. Secondly, it will not last long enough; it stops at AD 2000. I suppose this seems a long way ahead to our younger members, who do not know how time flies. Let them "wait till" they come to forty year." 2000 AD will be here before they know it. Nevertheless, I use the table in one section of the Athenaeum and mean to use it elsewhere. But in the classics it seemed better to put on the backs of the books a mark which everybody could understand at a glance, the usual date, 1886, 1494, etc. With our system of charg-

> ing the four figures cause no delay, and the greater clumsiness of the mark when used as a call number is compensated by its greater intelligibility on the shelf.[7]

John P. Comaromi's comments on the issue about a century after Cutter's are no less interesting: "Of course, the future lay in wait behind a bush; the alphabet runs out at AD 2000. Biscoe, however, trusted that the problems of the future would be solved by its citizens-only occasionally a misplaced trust."[8] Lehnus said pretty much the same thing: "Biscoe was not concerned that his table would reach its limit with the letter Z in the year 1999, and commented that before this limit was reached someone would have devised a better scheme."[9] No view could have been more in tune with the scientific and progressive spirit, a spirit that imbued Biscoe. Indeed, it is likely that the next century will have a concept and form of book number quite unlike what we know. It is, therefore, of little profit to dwell at length on this limitation of inadequate notation. In fact, the limitation allowed the alphabet to be distributed in a way comensurate with the literature it was devised to organize. The first limitation, that the meaning of the number was not self-evident, has no force. Like many another librarian down the ages, Cutter underestimated the strength and tenacity of the human mind. For if the author cannot be inferred from the chronological book number, certainly the year of publication can be deciphered as if by reflex action after modest experience, and the table can be committed to memory easily.

Regarding the limit of 2000 AD, if the system survives unsuperceded or replaced, it can certainly and easily be extended by any of the methods employed by Ranganathan for hospitality in the array of classes or more easily by making Z as a sectorizing digit:

ZA	2000-2009
ZB	2010-2019
ZC	2020-2029

and so on.

The operation of this simple system normally poses no particular difficulty. The digit B stands for the first millenium AD. It entails that three digits will have to be added to the letter B to represent any particular year of the period. For example:

1	AD	B001
100	AD	B100
240	AD	B240
555	AD	B555

C denotes the next five centuries (1000 to 1499 AD). To transcribe any particular year falling in this span of time, subtract 1000 (the starting point of the period) from the year and append the result to C. For example, 1235 AD will be denoted as C235 (1235 minus 1000). Similarly, some other years of this period will be denoted as follows:

1000	AD	(1000 minus 1000)	C000
1001	AD	(1001 minus 1000)	C001
1200	AD	(1200 minus 1000)	C200
1499	AD	(1499 minus 1000)	C499

The letters D, E, and F represent a century each, namely the 16th, 17th, and 18th centuries respectively. Of these centuries any particular year can be transcribed by adding two Indo-Arabic digits from the end of the century number to that particular century digit. For example:

1500	D00
1501	D01
1526	D26
1602	E02
1610	E10
1799	F99

From G (i.e., the 19th century) onwards every letter denotes a decade. This means that any particular year of the 19th or 20th centuries can be denoted by adding one digit (the particular year figure of the decade) to the single letter standing for that decade. For example:

1800	G0
1801	G1
1809	G9
1980	Y0
1987	Y7
1990	Z0
1999	Z9

Consequently, the years most frequently used are denoted by two digits resulting in an obvious brevity and a simple notation. There are difficulties, inevitably. Biscoe admitted that certain problems were unavoidable, the foremost being the occasional difficulty of determining the date of publication of the first edition of a work. As a last resort, when only the decade or century could be given with a degree of certainty, he [Biscoe] recommended assigning a letter only.[10] For example, if a book lacking a year of publication is thought to have been published sometime during the 1950s, then it could be numbered as F5; and a book supposed to have been published, say, between 1890 and 1899 may be given a temporary book number P, pending discovery of the true year and eliminating the need to erase a hasty figure only to rewrite the whole. Granted that such a solution is not perfect and is wearing, but it is needed everywhere, especially in those places where the publishing industry is not well developed.

What follow now are a few problems sure to crop up, and their solutions:

(1) In the case of a book reprinted many times or available in many versions, the year of the first publication of the original version may be taken as the gathering point for the work. It will bring together the original book and all its versions.

(2) To bring the different editions of a work together on the shelves, for the later editions the year of the first edition may be taken as the publication year for the book number.

(3) In the case of a multi-volume work whose different volumes are published in different years, the year of the first volume is to be taken as the book number for all the volumes.

(4) Similarly, the host and associated works in the form of supplements, adaptations, translations, and even commentaries, the publication year may be taken as that of the host work.

(5) In the case of two or more works being published in the same year in the same class, the book numbers may be differentiated by adding a lower case letter to the later book numbers. For example:

Library Classification by J. Mills 1962
Library Classification by B.I. Palmer 1962

The following classification and book numbers will be generated:

025.4 025.4
W2 W2a

Similarly, a third work on classification published in 1962 would get the book number W2b. Thus, a, b, etc. may be termed the "accession part of the year number"-according to Ranganathan terminology. The probability of the use of this device has enormously multiplied in the current literature proliferation.

Lehnus pointed out that "Biscoe made no mention of how to distinguish between two books written on the same subject and published in the same year" and suggested that "logically they would first be arranged by subject, then by year, and lastly by author."[11] By this suggestion the aforementioned two works will get the call numbers 025.4 W2M and 025.4 W2P.

Comes the test: how are we to handle book numbers for works written before the Christian era? The time, of course, has to be regarded as being negative. Thus, if books published between 1000 BC and 1 BC are arranged according to their year of publication, they will be arranged in the sequence of earlier year coming before later year. But how to do it? If we were to follow the normal practice, we would transcribe the dates as follows:

A0277	for	27	BC
A030	for	30	BC
A275	for	275	BC
A999	for	999	BC

But, clearly, with such a system earlier years fall later on the shelf. This cannot be allowed, nor thought to be helpful for anyone. The problem was raised in the October, 1893, issue of *Library Notes*, an issue devoted to book numbers. The editor wondered what to do with works of classical literature which were abundantly present in American libraries in those days. Three methods were suggested. Of the three, the first two may be termed as practicing the method of complements:

(1) The first method is a rather complicated one. To represent a particular BC year, the digit standing for unity (i.e., the last digit in the figure) is to be omitted, the remaining figure to stand for the century and decade is to be subtracted from 99; the resulting figure is to be appended to the digit A. To illustrate let us take the year 995 BC:

Omit the last digit	equals	99
Subtract in from 99	equals	00
Attach it to A	equals	A00

Hence, 999 BC is denoted as A00. In fact, any year from 990 BC to 999 BC will have the same notation. Similarly, for, say, 25 BC

Ignore the last digit	which is	2
Subtract 2 from 99	equals	97

Hence, it will be denoted as A97. Similarly, 299 BC will be A70. One difficulty with such a method is that its precision is not better than a decade. Consequently, two years falling in the same decade will get the same book number as shown above. But such a case will be a rare bird.

(2) The second method is comparatively more simple and precise. The given year is to be subtracted from 1000, the resulting figure to be converted from a negative to a positive value, e.g.:

400	BC	equals	A600
27	BC	equals	A973
5	BC	equals	A995

In this way the above book numbers will be arranged in the desired order on the later-in-time-principle.

(3) The third method is to write the figure and attach it to A. For example:

400	BC	A400
28	BC	A028
5	BC	A005

This leads to an order of A005, A028, and A400. It is unhelpful means, undeniably.

Biscoe time numbers were simple and are a pioneering method of the chronological arrangement of books. It is brief, as it should be. Being a pioneer, it appears to us as being rather primitive, as all original things are. His system was and is silent on many of the problems that modern works present to us. If one is silent on a problem, no solution is necessary. Nevertheless, we should not deny his system the honor of having been the first stone in a cathedral of thought. We close with the words that "Biscoe's time numbers are as efficacious as they are sound. They should be used more often."[12]

References

1. Comaromi, John P. *The Eighteen Editions of the Dewey Decimal Classification*. Albany, N.Y.: Forest press, 1976; p.
2. Dewey, Melvil. *Decimal Classification and Relative Index*. 2nd ed. Boston: Library Bureau, 1885; p. 44 (*quoted* by Comaromi, ibid. pp. 119-120)
3. Biscoe, W.S. "Chronological Arrangement on Shelves," *Library Journal* 10 (Sept.-Oct. 1885): 246-247
4. Biscoe, W.S. *ibid.*, p. 247
5. Dewey, Melvil. *Decimal Classification and Relative Index*. 4th ed. Boston: Library Bureau, 1891; p. 30 (*quoted* in Lehnus, p. 28)
6. Lehnus, Donald J. *Book Numbers*. p. 23
7. Cutter, C.A. "Author-tables for Greek and Latin Authors," *Library Journal* 11 (Aug.-Sept. 1886); 280
8. Comaromi, p. 46
9. Lehnus, p. 23
10. Comaromi, p. 46
11. Lehnus, p. 23
12. Comaromi, p. 47

CHAPTER 6

Brown's Extended Date Table

James Duff Brown, who exercised a formative role in early modern librarianship, was born on November 6, 1862, in Ediburgh into a working class family unusual in its love for art and thought, i.e., for music and for books. His formal education was sound but brief, ending at the age of 12. After four years of work in bookselling, he found an opening in the Mitchell Library of Glasgow. This growing library provided him the necessary training to engage an inquisitive and practical mind. At that time new libraries were being established under the library acts to provide employment and promotion avenues for young librarians within institutions that British leaders wished to promote. Brown became the first librarian of the Clerkenwell public library in a London parish. His appointment can now be seen as the inauguration of a new phase in British public library history. In 1905 he became the Borough Librarian of Islington. There he developed a public library service that came to be regarded at the time as a model of such service. His example, expertise, and crusades contributed much to modernize library outlook and services. One of his outstanding contributions was the introduction of open access to the shelves of British libraries. It was an idea he borrowed from the United States, even though he "manifested throughout his life a marked antipathy to American library methods and indeed to American librarianship generally," wrote W.A. Munford.

An engaging speaker and effective teacher, a library science educator, an administrator with an even hand, a prolific writer, a journalist (founder of the *Library World* in 1898), and a classificationist, he is well known for his enduring *Manual of Library Economy* (1903, 1907, 1920, 1931, 1949, 1961), which in its revised form is still a part of current library literature. The *Manual* is the epitome of his innovations in library management. It was for a long while the basic textbook for British public librarianship. Pragmatism, perhaps ensuing from his lack of a full formal education, is a marked characteristic of his life and work. In his ecumenical range of library science knowledge, he is usually classed with Melvil Dewey and S.R. Ranganathan. In British Library history he ranks with Edward Edwards (1812-1886) as "one of the makers of modern British librarianship." He died on February 26, 1914.

Brown wrote prolifically on classification at a time when classification studies in Britain did not attract the attention and intellect that it deserved. He produced at least three classification systems. The first was *Classification of Books in Libraries in Which Readers Are Allowed Access to the Shelves*. It was done in collaboration with John H. Quinn and published in 1885 in *The Library*—a journal to which Brown was a heavy contributor. His first scheme was followed by the Adjustable Classification, which, though it was based mostly upon the Quinn-Brown system (the earlier scheme), was essentially an eclectic work. The two systems would make no lasting mark in the practice of library classification. His Subject Classification, by which he is most known today in the classification area, was published in 1906. It remains the only complete general British classification. Brown's primary motive in producing a general classification was merely to design a British scheme free from the American bias of the DDC—a scheme he detested.

The Subject Classification was experimental and innovative. Methodologically, it proved to be a fiasco as it collocated subjects by what he called the method of attraction; he discarded the proven method of arranging the universe of knowledge into the disciplines that *study* subject. In essence his method of organization was to take a concrete entity and place with it all its associated processes, thus, say, the law of buildings would go with buildings—where also would be found keeping buildings clean, building buildings, photographing buildings, drawing buildings, and so on. One can see at once that such a system is intellectually flawed and fraught with practical difficulties. When taken to the extreme, some of the combinations of entity to process were surreal and others frankly embarrassing. The overall order of the classes was determined by his concept of the evolutionary sequence of entities, i.e., Matter, Force, Life, Mind, and Record. Translated into practice these become the Physical sciences (Matter and Force), the Biological sciences (Life), Philosophy and Religion (Mind), and History, Biography, and Literature (Record). Theory and practice were to be displayed alternately in a linear fashion. The second edition of the scheme was published in 1914, the third edition (revised by his nephew J.D. Stewart) in 1939. In the 1950s an estimated forty libraries in the United Kingdom were using the scheme, which is now dead or breathing shallowly-for want of revision if for no other reason. Arthur Maltby agrees with Eric de Grolier that Brown's scheme was good in the context of his time. Whatever the case, Brown's contribution to classification and indexing surely affected the thought of subsequent thinkers in this field. His influence on the great and revolutionary classificationist Ranganathan (1892-1972) is apparent, though it has not been acknowledged or explored.

Brown's other works on classification include his *Manual of Library Classification and Shelf Arrangement* (London: Library Supply Co., 1898) and *Library Classification and Cataloguing* (London:The Library Association, 1912). He devised two systems of book numbers, one alphabetical and the other chronological. Lacking any originality these are deservedly the least remembered of his contributions. As for his Date Table (the subject of this study), it made no conceptual or practical advances over the system of earlier writers on the subject.

Up to this point the subject of book numbers had remained in the hands of Americans; Brown seems to have been the first person outside America to invest much effort in the subject. He made a brief critical study of all the existing systems of book numbers as well as devising his chronological and alphabetical tables. His chronological book numbers system is labeled the Extended Date Table. As said earlier, the table has a span of 1450 to 2125 AD. Every year in the span can be designated by two lower case letters. In broad form his table follows:

1450-1475	aa-az	1710-1735	ka-kz
1476-1501	ba-bz	1736-1761	la-lz
1502-1527	ca-cz	1762-1787	ma-mz
1528-1553	da-dz	1788-1813	na-nz
1554-1579	ea-ez	1814-1839	oa-oz
1580-1605	fa-fz	1840-1865	pa-pz
1606-1631	ga-gz	1866-1891	qa-qz
1632-1657	ha-hz	1892-1917	ra-rz
1658-1683	ia-iz	1918-1943	sa-sz
1684-1709	ja-jz	1944-1969	ta-tz

1970-1995	ua-uz	2048-2073	xa-xz
1996-2021	va-uz	2074-2099	ya-yz
2022-2047	wa-wz	2100-2125	za-zz

The Full table is as follow:

1450	aa	1484	bi
1451	ab	1485	bj
1452	ac	1486	bk
1453	ad	1487	bl
1454	ae	1488	bm
1455	af	1489	bn
1456	ag	1490	bo
1457	ah	1491	bp
1458	ai	1492	bq
1459	aj	1493	br
1460	ak	1494	bs
1461	al	1495	bt
1462	am	1496	bu
1463	an	1497	bv
1464	ao	1498	bw
1465	ap	1499	bx
1466	aq	1500	by
1467	ar	1501	bz
1468	as	1502	ca
1469	at	1503	cb
1470	au	1504	cc
1471	av	1505	cd
1472	aw	1506	ce
1473	ax	1507	cf
1474	ay	1508	cg
1475	az	1509	ch
1476	ba	1510	ci
1477	bb	1511	cj
1478	bc	1512	ck
1479	bd	1513	cl
1480	be	1514	cm
1481	bf	1515	cn
1482	bg	1516	co
1483	bh	1517	cp

1518	cq	1559	ef
1519	cr	1560	eg
1520	cs	1561	eh
1521	ct	1562	ei
1522	cu	1563	ej
1523	cv	1564	ek
1524	cw	1565	el
1525	cx	1566	em
1526	cy	1567	en
1527	cz	1568	eo
1528	da	1569	ep
1529	db	1570	eq
1530	dc	1571	er
1531	dd	1572	es
1532	de	1573	et
1533	df	1574	eu
1534	dg	1575	ev
1535	dh	1576	ew
1536	di	1577	ex
1537	dj	1578	ey
1538	dk	1579	ez
1539	dl	1580	fa
1540	dm	1581	fb
1541	dn	1582	fc
1542	do	1583	fd
1543	dp	1584	fe
1544	dq	1585	ff
1545	dr	1586	fg
1546	ds	1587	fh
1547	dt	1588	fi
1548	du	1589	fj
1549	dv	1590	fk
1550	dw	1591	fl
1551	dx	1592	fm
1552	dy	1593	fn
1553	dz	1594	fo
1554	ea	1595	fp
1555	eb	1596	fq
1556	ec	1597	fr
1557	ed	1598	fs
1558	ee	1599	ft

1600	fu	1640	hi
1601	fv	1641	hj
1602	fw	1642	hk
1603	fx	1643	hl
1604	fy	1644	hm
1605	fz	1645	hn
1606	ga	1646	ho
1607	gb	1647	hp
1608	gc	1648	hq
1609	gd	1649	hr
1610	ge	1650	hs
1611	gf	1651	ht
1612	gg	1652	hu
1613	gh	1653	hv
1614	gi	1654	hw
1615	gj	1655	hx
1616	gk	1656	hy
1617	gl	1657	hz
1618	gm	1658	ia
1619	gn	1659	ib
1620	go	1660	ic
1621	gp	1661	id
1622	gq	1662	ie
1623	gr	1663	if
1624	gs	1664	ig
1625	gt	1665	ih
1626	gu	1666	ii
1627	gv	1667	ij
1628	gw	1668	ik
1629	gx	1669	il
1630	gy	1670	im
1631	gz	1671	in
1632	ha	1672	io
1633	hb	1673	ip
1634	hc	1674	iq
1635	hd	1675	ir
1636	he	1676	is
1637	hf	1677	it
1638	hg	1678	iu
1639	hh	1679	iv

1680	iw	1720	kk
1681	ix	1721	kl
1682	iy	1722	km
1683	iz	1723	kn
1684	ja	1724	ko
1685	jb	1725	kp
1686	jc	1726	kq
1687	jd	1727	kr
1688	je	1728	ks
1689	jf	1729	kt
1690	jg	1730	ku
1691	jh	1731	kv
1692	ji	1732	kw
1693	jj	1733	kx
1694	jk	1734	ky
1695	jl	1735	kz
1696	jm	1736	la
1697	jn	1737	lb
1698	jo	1738	lc
1699	jp	1739	ld
1700	jq	1740	le
1701	jr	1741	lf
1702	js	1742	lg
1703	jt	1743	lh
1704	ju	1744	li
1705	jv	1745	lj
1706	jw	1746	lk
1707	jx	1747	ll
1708	jy	1748	lm
1709	jz	1749	ln
1710	ka	1750	lo
1711	kb	1751	lp
1712	kc	1752	lq
1713	kd	1753	lr
1714	ke	1754	ls
1715	kf	1755	lt
1716	kg	1756	lu
1717	kh	1757	lv
1718	ki	1758	lw
1719	kj	1759	lx

1760	ly	1800	nm
1761	lz	1801	nn
1762	ma	1802	no
1763	mb	1803	np
1764	mc	1804	nq
1765	md	1805	nr
1766	me	1806	ns
1767	mf	1807	nt
1768	mg	1808	nu
1769	mh	1809	nv
1770	mi	1810	nw
1771	mj	1811	nx
1772	mk	1812	ny
1773	ml	1813	nz
1774	mm	1814	oa
1775	mn	1815	ob
1776	mo	1816	oc
1777	mp	1817	od
1778	mq	1818	oe
1779	mr	1819	of
1780	ms	1820	og
1781	mt	1821	oh
1782	mu	1822	oi
1783	mv	1823	oj
1784	mw	1824	ok
1785	mx	1825	ol
1786	my	1826	om
1787	mz	1827	on
1788	na	1828	oo
1789	nb	1829	op
1790	nc	1830	oq
1791	nd	1831	or
1792	ne	1832	os
1793	nf	1833	ot
1794	ng	1834	ou
1795	nh	1835	ov
1796	ni	1836	ow
1797	nj	1837	ox
1798	nk	1838	oy
1799	nl	1839	oz

1840	pa	1880	qo
1841	pb	1881	qp
1842	pc	1882	qq
1843	pd	1883	qr
1844	pe	1884	qs
1845	pf	1885	qt
1846	pg	1886	qu
1847	ph	1887	qv
1848	pi	1888	qw
1849	pj	1889	qx
1850	pk	1890	qy
1851	pl	1891	qz
1852	pm	1892	ra
1853	pn	1893	rb
1854	po	1894	rc
1855	pp	1895	rd
1856	pq	1896	re
1857	pr	1897	rf
1858	ps	1898	rg
1859	pt	1899	rh
1860	pu	1900	ri
1861	pv	1901	rj
1862	pw	1902	rk
1863	px	1903	rl
1864	py	1904	rm
1865	pz	1905	rn
1866	qa	1906	ro
1867	qb	1907	rp
1868	qc	1908	rq
1869	qd	1909	rr
1870	qe	1910	rs
1871	qf	1911	rt
1872	qg	1912	ru
1873	qh	1913	rv
1874	qi	1914	rw
1875	qj	1915	rx
1876	qk	1916	ry
1877	ql	1917	rz
1878	qm	1918	sa
1879	qn	1919	sb

1920	sc	1960	tq
1921	sd	1961	tr
1922	se	1962	ts
1923	sf	1963	tt
1924	sg	1964	tu
1925	sh	1965	tv
1926	si	1966	tw
1927	sj	1967	tx
1928	sk	1968	ty
1929	sl	1969	tz
1930	sm	1970	ua
1931	sn	1971	ub
1932	so	1972	uc
1933	sp	1973	ud
1934	sq	1974	ue
1935	sr	1975	uf
1936	ss	1976	ug
1937	st	1977	uh
1938	su	1978	ui
1939	sv	1979	uj
1940	sw	1980	uk
1941	sx	1981	ul
1942	sy	1982	um
1943	sz	1983	un
1944	ta	1984	uo
1945	tb	1985	up
1946	tc	1986	uq
1947	td	1987	ur
1948	te	1988	us
1949	tf	1989	ut
1950	tg	1990	uu
1951	th	1991	uv
1952	ti	1992	uw
1953	tj	1993	ux
1954	tk	1994	uy
1955	tl	1995	uz
1956	tm	1996	va
1957	tn	1997	vb
1958	to	1998	vc
1959	tp	1999	vd

2000	ve	2040	ws
2001	vf	2041	wt
2002	vg	2042	wu
2003	vh	2043	wv
2004	vi	2044	ww
2005	vj	2045	wx
2006	vk	2046	wy
2007	vl	2047	wz
2008	vm	2048	xa
2009	vn	2049	xb
2010	vo	2050	xc
2011	vp	2051	xd
2012	vq	2052	xe
2013	vr	2053	xf
2014	vs	2054	xg
2015	vt	2055	xh
2016	vu	2056	xi
2017	vv	2057	xj
2018	vw	2058	xk
2019	vx	2059	xl
2020	vy	2060	xm
2021	vz	2061	xn
2022	wa	2062	xo
2023	wb	2063	xp
2024	wc	2064	xq
2025	wd	2065	xr
2026	we	2066	xs
2027	wf	2067	xt
2028	wg	2068	xu
2029	wh	2069	xv
2030	wi	2070	xw
2031	wj	2071	xx
2032	wk	2072	xy
2033	wl	2073	xz
2034	wm	2074	ya
2035	wn	2075	yb
2036	wo	2076	yc
2037	wp	2077	yd
2038	wq	2078	ye
2039	wr	2079	yf

2080	yg	2102	zc
2081	yh	2103	zd
2082	yi	2104	ze
2083	yj	2105	zf
2084	yk	2106	zg
2085	yl	2107	zh
2086	ym	2108	zi
2087	yn	2109	zj
2088	yo	2110	zk
2089	yp	2111	zl
2090	yq	2112	zm
2091	yr	2113	zn
2092	ys	2114	zo
2093	yt	2115	zp
2094	yu	2116	zq
2095	yv	2117	zr
2096	yw	2118	zs
2097	yx	2119	zt
2098	yy	2120	zu
2099	yz	2121	zv
2100	za	2122	zw
2101	zb	2123	zx
		2124	zy
		2125	zz

The table could not be less mnemonic; every time a book number is to be assigned the classifier must consult the table. A.D. 1450 was chosen as the starting point because it comes at the putative beginning of printing from movable type (in the Western world). So the table is primarily for printed books. Brown advised that for manuscripts a similar table could be constructed using capital letters. We would like to say that Brown had an expansive mind, inasmuch as he moved far into the future in his table, much farther than any of his predecessors. The fact of the matter is that squaring the number of letters of the Roman alphabet produces 676 years denotable uniquely by a two-letter combination, and 1449 added to 676 give us 2125—the point where Brown rested from his labor on the table. If the alphabet had four more letters, Brown would have bumped along up to 2349, stopped, smiled, and gone on to something else.

Like many another chronological book number system it is silent on many of the problems that classifiers face if they employ such a system. It does have a device for bringing together all copies of the same book, which is done by attaching to the symbol a dash (—), and then 1, 2, 3 and so on for the first, second, third, and nth copy of the particular item. For example, ux-2 and ux-3 denote the second and third copies respectively of a book published in 1993. The system does not appear to have any advantage over the Biscoe system (other than a briefer but un-mnemonic notation), yet it inherits all of its disadvantages. It now occurs to us that librarianship has an almost unblemished record of devising less round wheels than those that were handed down to it by preceding generations.

References

Source material

Brown, J.D. *Subject Classification.* 3rd ed., rev. by J.D. Stewart. London: Grafton, 1939; sec. 30-40; pp. 26-32

Further readings

Butcher, S.J. "Brown Classification," *in Encyclopedia of Library and Information Science.* New York: Marcel Dekker, 1970; v. 3; pp. 367-371

Maltby, Arthur, *Sayers's Manual of Classification for Librarians.* 5th ed. London: Andre Deutsch, 1975; pp. 128-131

Munford, W.A. "Brown, James Duff," *in ALA World Encyclopedia of Library and Information Services,* ed. by Robert Wedgeworth. Chicago: ALA, 1980; pp. 101-102

Munford, W.A. *James Duff Brown 1862-1914: Portrait of a Library Pioneer.* London: the Library Association, 1968; 101p.

CHAPTER 7

Colon Book Numbers

It is a matter of pride for all Indians, whether they know it or not, that in library science India has blazed a trail for the library world. Dr. Shiyali Ramamrita Ranganathan (1892-1972), probably the greatest of Indian library statesmen, revived a part of the tradition of ancient India to attract scholars from lands beyond its borders to learn what India had divined of the world. Ranganathan was born on August 12, 1892, to a Brahmin family in the village of Shiyali in the then Madras Presidency. Being born in a poor family steeped in religion and orthodoxy, his life was strewn with economic difficulties and aggravated by poor health. The early death of his father N. Ramamritam Ayyar (1866-1898) was another burden to bear. If Ranganathan did not have bad luck, he would have had no luck at all. Wading his way through hardships, he passed his MA in mathematics in 1916 and started teaching in colleges affiliated with Madras University. He loved both teaching and mathematics. The hours of his life fell away easily.

Suddenly, in 1924, he discovered librarianship, which in those days was not a career for the learned or ambitious. As stipulated in his appointment into librarianship, he went to England for training, whence he returned in 1925. After that, neither he nor librarianship were the same. The prevailing library science theory and teaching did not satisfy a mind steeped in mathematics. Nevertheless, he had been much impressed by the variety and extent of the library service provided to almost every element of the British community. When he came back to India, his mind could barely contain the ideas that swarmed there. He set himself two tasks: (1) imparting improved and wide library facilities to every Indian, and (2) making library science true to the second half of its name by writing it anew on rigidly scientific principles. From the start, he engaged himself in working toward the goals he had set for himself. For the colossal task a band of dedicated men was needed. In 1928 he founded the Madras Library Association, and the Association instituted a library school to produce trained and able librarians.

The foremost need was to create a social awakening for the value of libraries, scholars, and laymen alike that a library is a repository of culture and an apparatus for racial memory, a view promoted by Carl Sagan in his television series "Cosmos." Libraries are an indispensible part in the elimination of ignorance and its consequent poverty. He created a library consciousness among his countrymen. He was, indeed, a one-man library movement in India, even more so that Dewey was in the United States. He planned and worked hard for an integrated system, i.e., a network of libraries for all of India. After several failures he succeeded in getting library legislation enacted in the then Madras province. Now library facilities are provided legislatively in eight Indian states. This is only a partial fulfillment of his dream of a public library system in India. But it will come.

The crusader in him never weakened the scientist that he was. His deliberations on the theory of library science altered its very face. In his first book, the *Five Laws of Library Science* (1931), he gave library science for the first time a cogent philosophy and norm. The laws propounded by him are as true as any of the social sciences. By induction, deduction, and any other intellectual method that would suit his purpose, he carved out as simple corollaries of his laws, the principles and implications for every branch of the discipline, and wrote upon each. His Colon Classification (published first in 1933 and now in its 7th edition [1987]) has been considered as the greatest breakthrough in bibliographic classification since Dewey published his first edition in 1876.

The principles of the Colon Classification are taught in many of the library schools of the world and practised widely in India. The full volume of his writing amounts to sixty books and two thousand articles! His work has gained so much acceptance that it forms the very bedrock of much new research being carried out in library science. It is hard to imagine a library science without Ranganathan; certainly many scholars and organizations have suggested the same. Some have even called his year of production the "Ranganathan Age." One does not have to stretch his mind to imagine the reverence with which he is held in India.

In 1945 Ranganathan joined Benares Hindu University on the invitation of Dr. S. Radhakrishnan, then its vice-chancellor, and later president of the Republic of India. In 1947 on the request of Sir Maurice Gwyer he took charge of the library science department of the University of Delhi. There for the first time in the British Commonwealth he instituted master and research degrees in library science after overcoming doubtful opposition (at that time library science was not considered worthy of higher academic pursuits).

By the late 1940s, Ranganathan had become a familiar name in library circles, and he had also become the President of the Indian Library Association (which helps to give name recognition). To the Association Ranganathan gave a thorough professional character and outlook from 1944 to 1953. He died September 27, 1972, at Bangalore after a brief illness.

Eventually and unusually honors came to him who deserved them richly by his acts and achievements.

Like his class numbers Ranganathan's system of book numbers is also faceted. it takes into consideration the language, form, year of publication, supplements, volumes, and copies of a book. Criticism of a work is also considered in the formula. Provision has been made to make each facet distinctive. The facet formula (with indicators) follows:

[L] [F] [Y] [A] . [V] - [S] ; [C] : g [EVN]

The symbols denote language, form, year, accession part of the year number, volume, supplement, copy, and criticism (denoted by g) and the evaluation number in the order given.

The first criterion of a book number is language, followed by the form of document. Within a given language and form the documents are arranged by year of publication. The accession part of the year number is a device to individualize further (if there are two or more books published in the same year, and in the same language and form). Evaluation numbers distinguish whether there are two or more critical works or commentaries on a given book still undistinguished by language, form, and year of publication. The further facets of the formula for book numbers are devices to collocate parts, supplements, volumes, editions, and criticism in the case of semi classics all to keep the contingent works with the original work, i.e., to bring the host and the associated works together. There is no device in the CC to keep an adaptation and abridgment with the host work. As for the adaptation, that is fine, but abridgments of a work are better placed with a work than away from it.

The length or the apparent complexity of the facet formula should not lead to the impression that CC book numbers are lenthier or more complicated than others. Contrary to such an impression, most of the book numbers derived consist of two digits only-both representing the chronological facet. Other facets, such as language, form, volume, supplement, or copy number are required in a minority of cases. Such brevity in the CC book number stems from two conditions. Firstly, the facet formula for the book number takes into consideration the oddities of a document. The majority of documents, being in a normal form, do not contain all the facets possible. Secondly, the principle of Favored Category has been made use of in the case of a favored language and favored form of document. Such a practice secures brevity in book number without harming its efficacy or coextensiveness. And only in extreme cases (which are rare) may the full facet formula be used. In fact, Ranganathan claimed that in more than 90 percent of the books the book number will have only the year number.[1] His assertion can be easily verified by any experienced Colon classifier or by a sample of documents for length of their book numbers. Ranganathan further justified each facet in the book number with the claim that "each facet has been introduced only on the basis of actual experience gained by observing the reaction of the readers while in the stack room and noting some of their remarks."[2] His assertion is proved true by the precision with which the host and its associated documents file together. Another major advantage of the Colon book number system is that with a little practice one need not consult the table every time a number is assigned. In a well-built chronological table, one commits to memory even at the first effort to use it. Even language and form numbers linger in the memory after a brief practice. Other facets are taken from the book itself. Thus, building book numbers for use with the Colon Classification is expeditious in the majority of cases. It saves the time of the staff, which satisfies the Fourth Law of Library Science. This is hardly possible in systems coding the author's name into numerals.

Facets

1. Language facet [L]: It is a myth that in the Colon Classification documents are sub-arranged by their year of publication. The

first grouping of books within a given ultimate class is by the language of the document. This first facet secures collocation of linguistic groups. Since the majority of readers know but one language, or one language well enough to learn profitably through reading it, they will find all their relevant books together. The book number results from the putting of the language isolate number as taken from Chapter 5 of the Schedules (found there on pages 2.26-2.27 of CC-7 (1987) found here in Appendix I of this chapter). It is the first facet in the book number. But in the majority of documents it need not be added, specifically in the following kinds:

(a) Documents in the most favored language of the library.
The favored language of a library is determined on the basis of literary warrant. It is the language of the majority of documents; it is not any arbitrarily chosen language that the librarian happens to prefer. It is the official language of country in which the majority of the intellectual and administrative work is done. Thus, the majority of documents will be without a language number, still they will constitute a linguistic group that files together.

(b) Documents falling in main class O Literature will not get the [L] facet if the language of the literature and that of the book is the same. In such cases since the language facet is represented in the class number, thereis no need for repetition. In the case of what Ranganathan calls Language Inequality, the [L] facet will have to be added even though the exposition of the work is in the favoured language of the library. For example, *Hamlet* in, say, French is a case of language inequality; so are Gunther Grass's works in English or French. For example, in India, English is taken as the favored language. But if a book on the history of Hindi literature is written in the English language, the language nu ber will have to be added. This rule also applies to the main class P Linguistics of the Colon Classification.

(c) Also in the case of periodical publications the language number need not be added. Ranganathan thought (erroneously) that the language of the periodical would be that of the country. Since the geographical facet would already have been added in the facet formula for periodical publications there was no need for additing the language facet. But this rule may raise problems in multilingual countries like Canada. The weak generalization can be made that the language facet will only be required in the book number in the case of foreign works except for the language and literature classes.

2. Form facet [F]: This is the physical body of the book—its outer container. The physical exposition, or organization, of the intellecutal or ideational contents of books has been far ranging in varitey since the very inception of the book. Some works are all illustrations, others are tables and charts solely. Some non-literary works may use verse for the exposition of the text. Ranganathan has enumerated more than sixty forms of exposition that a book may take in Chapter 02 of the Schedules at page 2.3 of CC-7 (1987) (given here as Appendix 2 of this chapter). It is felt that his catalog of forms is not exhaustive. The function of the form facet is to bring together all the books in the same form within a given language. Again by using the principle of favored category, in the favored form of the documents the form facet may be omitted. In virtually all libraries today, the prose form is the favored form as the vast majority of codex books are written in this mode of expression. Therefore, for books written in prose the form number may be suppressed. Similarly, in a microfilm library the form for microfilm may be omitted. Thus the majority of documents in a library are without form number. For literary works the forms given from w1 to w7 need not be added as they have already been made part of the class number.
3. Year number [Y]: This facet is the core of the book number. No book number can be without it. Professor A.P. Srivastava aptly calls it the major-domo facet.[3] It consists in transcribing the year of publication of the book into a mixed code of Roman capitals and Indo-arabic numbers. For the book number a special conversion table was devised by Ranganathan and given at page 1.13 of the Rules part of the Colon Classification, 6th ed., and given here as follows:

A	Before 1880	F	1920-1929	L	1970-1979
B	1880-1889	G	1930-1939	M	1980-1989
C	1890-1899	H	1940-1949	N	1990-1999
D	1900-1909	J	1950-1959	P	2000-2009
E	1910-1919	K	1960-1969	Q	2010-2019

R	2020-2029	V	2060-2069	ZA	2100-2109
S	2030-2039	W	2070-2079	ZB	2110-2119
T	2040-2049	X	2080-2089	ZC	2120-2129
U	2050-2059	Y	2090-2099		

The letters I and O have not been used to avoid confusing them with 1 and 0.

For example, the individual years given below will be denoted as follows:

1900	D0	1928	F8
1920	F0	1960	K0
1921	F1	1969	K9

But 1857 will be denoted as A857

This table was devised on the proportionate allocation of digits. Not only this, it is a fine example of proportionate allocation of notation among subjects.[4] With two digits, one Roman capital and the other an Indo-arabic numeral, any year from 1880 to 2099 can be briefly denoted. Years beyond the latter and before the former will require more notation: Several letters for the years beyond 2099 and several numbers for the years before 1880. In the table, from B onward each letter represents a specific decade. The exact year can be denoted by adding any digit 0 through 9 to the decade digit. As far as a two-digited year number is concerned, this table is useful only for a limited period-1880 through 2099 AD. It is, of course, sufficient for several more generations to come. Nevertheless, Ranganathan (perhaps a bit too high-mindedly) felt that it is "too selfish of the present generation to manage with two digits and leave the later generations to have three or more digits for the year number."[5] While Ranganathans argument is more than marginally moral, Walter Stanley Biscoe, when confronted with the same worry, thought that future generations will solve their own problems.[6] It is, in short, not wise to starve oneself to death, childless, for the benefit of unborn children and grand-children. But Ranganathan listened to his own counsel and abandoned the use of the special chronological table, and used instead the general one meant for the time facet in the class number. This table is given in Chapter 3 of the Rules portion of the Colon Classification on page 2.7 (and in Appendix 3 of this chapter). In the general table each year is denoted by one Roman capital and two

Indo-arabic numerals. For example, the individual years below will be denoted as given:

1757	L57	1921	N21
1887	M87	1928	N28
1900	N00	1960	N60
1920	N20	1969	N69

Both tables are still in use, the special table seeming to be the more popular. Classifiers have the option to use either table. The special table is recommended for its brevity.

If the date of publication of a document is spread over several years, the initial year is to be used for constructing the book number. For example, if two volumes of a work were published in 1967 and 1968 respectively, then K7 will be used as the core of the book number for each volume. Similarly, if a supplement is issued later, the year number for constructing its book number will be that of the parent book.

4. Accession part of the year number [A]: It may also happen that the library acquires two or more books on the same specific subject in the same year. In such cases the year number alone will most likely fail to individualize the book. To carry out the complete individualization, an Indo-arabic digit 1,2,3..(n-1) is added to the year number for the second, third, fourth, and nth books respectively that were published in the same year. Here n is an integer, not a decimal fraction. For example, if there are three books published on classification in 1967, then each will have a call number as follows:

   2 ; 5 K7
   2 ; 5 K71
   2 ; 5 K72

   For a 15th such book the call number will be 2 ; 5 K714. It may be noted that if in the above case the language and the form of the three books are different, then the accession part of the year number need not be added. For example, let us assume that of the three books one is in French, while the second one is in lecture form, and the third is a prose English book on classification; then the above call numbers will take the following forms respectively:

2 ; 5	122 K7
2 ; 5	p^1 K7
2 ; 5	K7

Since in this case the documents get individualized by virtue of having a different language or form, there is no need to add the [A], which is not truly a facet but rather a device for distinguishing items otherwise similar. [A] is to be added only when L, F, and Y taken together fail to individualize a document. It may also be said that the accession part of the year number is to be added when the library acquires two books similar in every respect, not when two books are published in the same year whether or not the library acquires both.

To know whether or not a book requires the accession part of the year number entails work. There is no method to determine this other than to check the shelflist or classified catalog. Therefore, the classifier will have to refer constantly to a library catalog, except in those rare cases where the classifier knows for certain that no book has already been acquired on the same subject published in the same language, form, and year. There will be problems if the catalog used is not kept up-to-date in a timely fashion. The addition of this part of the book number is likely to take more time than the addition of all the genuine facets taken together.

The first three facets in the book number are always there, whether they are coded for or not. No book can be without them. But the facets for volume and supplement are inherent only to the books issued in more than one installment. Since the majority of books are complete in one volume, most books will not require these facets. The need for keeping supplements and volumes together is obvious and is as Ranganathan wrote: "The need for indicating volume number and supplement number is inherent."[7] The need for adding a copy number is incidental to a particular library.

5. Volume number [V]: It may be pointed out that Ranganathan did not consider it necessary to keep all volumes of a work together. In fact, his standards for keeping different volumes of a work together are rigorous.[8] If it is decided to keep the volumes together, then it is done by adding 1, 2, 3, etc. for the first, second, third, and so on volumes after the year number of the accession part of the year number as the case may be. The indicator symbol for the volume number is a dot. For example, for a multi-volumed work published in 1961:

K6.1	1st volume
K6.2	2nd volume
K61.1	1st volume
K61.2	2nd vlume
....	....
K61.10	10th volume
K61.n	nth volume

Here the n is an integer, not a decimal fraction.

6. Supplement [S]: Inevitably there is a need to keep together a work and its addenda issued subsequently from time to time. The digit added for the supplement is known as the supplement number. It consists in adding 1, 2, 3...n with the indicator symbol "—" (dash) preceding the supplement. In the case of a supplement the L, F, and Y, V will be the same as that of the original volume. It will keep the supplement with its parent volume. For example,

   K61.1
   K61.2

   If the supplement is to the first volume, then the supplements will get the following numbers:

   K61.1-1
   K61.1-2
   K61.1-n
   K61.2

   But if the supplement is for both volumes, then it may be treated as the supplement of the last volume. It is only a device to keep the supplement after the last volume. The supplement number is to be read as an integer.

7. Copy number [C]: If the library acquires more than one copy of a book, the copies are invariably kept together. In this case the copy number is heralded by a semicolon after the supplement number. The copy number consists in putting 1,2,3 for the second, third, and fourth copies of a book respectively. For example, the 11th copy of a book will get the book number:

   K61 ; 10

   or

   K61-1 ; 10 as the case may be.

   The copy number is to be read as an integer. It may be said that if the copies of a book are placed in different sections of the library (as one in reference and one in the circulating collection), there is no need of giving the copy number except when a particular collection holds more than one copy.

8. Criticism number : [g]: If a book attracts a book on itself, the critical and other associated books should be kept with the host book. Such books having critical books and commentaries on them are termed as "pseudo-classics" by Ranganathan (though we ourselves would not leap to say what is or is not a classic)[9]. In such cases the critical work of the host book is given the class number of the host book. The criticism letter "g" is added after the copy number in the book number (which is strange: after which copy does the criticism go?). This criticism number is treated the same as the posteriorizing of the energy common isolate occurring in the class number. Here it has been applied to the book number with equal facility. For exxample, take a critique of Hardy's Number Theory published in 1932. The critique was published in 1982, say:

   B13 G2 : g

9. Accession part of the criticism number or evaluation number [EVN]: If a work invites more than two commentaries on it, then to distinguish them further evaluation numbers 1, 2, 3, and so may be added to the criticism number for the second, third, and fourth books, and so on respectively. For example, for a second critique of Hardy's *Number Theory*, published in 1982:

   B13 G2 : g1

   The accession part of the criticism number need not be added if the book is distinguished by language or form. For example, another book on Hardy's Number Theory in the Hindi language might get the following number:

   B13
   152G2 : g

   Here the accession part of the criticism number has not been added because the book already has become distinct from other book by virtue of being in a different language. Therefore, no accession part has been added to it—since it is only an individualizing agent. Again, the comments made in the case of the accession part of the year number are applicable here.

10. Various editions of a work: A regular objection raised against Ranganathan's system of book number is that it separates a new edition of a work from its previous editions. Actually, there seems to be no requirement to collocate the old and newer editions of a work; they are kept together, after all, in the catalog. Why do they have to be kept together on the shelf? In fact, works are rewritten only to incorporate the new developments of the field they treat, thus to bring them to currency. It will be, therefore, more appropriate and useful if a new edition is placed amongst its contemporaries and without regard to its previous incarnations. If in the previous life, one was a gnat, and is now human, it would avail us little to shelve the human with the gnat. So it is with editions of works. After all, a work is read and estimated in relation to other works published on the same subject during a temporally contingent span. A new edition of a textbook is in competition with its temporal cousins, not in competition with its distant ancestor or with own self. If, however, a library decides to place together all the editions of a work, then the new edition may be treated as a copy of the old edition. But in such a case, the year of publication of the new edition is to be treated as the copy number. For example, suppose a book was published in 1962 and a new edition arrived in 1967, then the new edition may get the following book number:

    K2 ; K7

    If another edition of it comes in 1970, then instead of repeating all the notations for the intermediary editions only the first edition and the last edition need to be denoted:

    K2 ; L0

    This will come after K2 ; K7, and at the same time all the editions of the work will come together in the sequence of their publication dates. It will also secure brevity and avoid unnecessary complications in the book number.
11. Ordinal value of digits: In the Colon Classification book number system no new species of characters have been used, though the functions assigned to the species and indicator digits are not the same as normally understood. The ordinal value of each species and indicator characters are different. The ordinal value

of each species has been refixed for book numbers so as to secure the required sequence. The different species used here are as follows:

Roman capitals A to Z (except I and 0) for decade numbers	24
Roman lowercase a-z (except i, l, and o)	23
Indo-arabic numerals used variously 0-9	10
Indicator characters . — ; :	4

The total number of characters is 61. The ordinal value assigned to each is as follow,[10] as arranged in the ascending sequence:

A-Z, a-z .—;: 0-9

Here the Roman capital letters have the least ordinal value (by ordinal we mean the power to determine position between the 1st and 25th elements of whatever is measured). Those of the Indo-arabic numerals have the highest. No principle of inversion has been followed. The value of indicator digits has been fixed in the ascending order as they appear in the facet formula of the book number. Somewhat puzzling and not particularly intelligent rules have been laid down in the case of the accession part of a year and the criticism number, volume number and copy number. In all these casese Indo-arabic numerals have been employed. It has been postulated that if they consist of two or more digits, then they are to be considered as integers. There seems no harm if all the digits in the volume, copy, and accession part of the criticism number are treated as integers always. But the difficulty arises in the case of the accession part of the year number. The first Indo-arabic digit in this case is a decimal fraction, while the rest are integers. For example, for a third book published on a subject in the year 1967, the book number will be K72. For the 12th book published on the subject in the same year, the number will be K711. It is necessary that the latter book should file later, so it has to be regarded as an integer, thus giving K711 more ordinal value than K72. For the 12th book published on the subject in the same year, the number will be K711. From which stems the rule. This complexity could have been avoided by using group notation as in the case of the work number [P4] of main class O literature in the Colon Classification, but even that method has some uncomfortable complexities, and is lengthier. A little practice will train the mind to make the required distinction between the fractional and integral values. But is is not a happy situation.

Some more examples will illustrate the ordinal value of the digits:

History of librarians in India in the 19th century

2"v44'M

Book number for several books on the above topic:

K7	Published in 1967
153K7	In Hindi published in 1967

Since the ordinal value of Indo-arabic numerals is greater than that of the Roman capitals, the sequence of the two book numbers will be as given above. A third work comes along:

p1K7	Lectures published in 1967

The ordinal value of a lowercase Roman letter is more than Z but less than 0-9; therefore, p1 will fall between K7 and 153K7. The sequence will be as follows:

K7
p1K7
153K7

If the lectures published in 1967 are in Hindi, the book number will be

153p1K7

A few more examples will illustrate the structure and sequence of book numbers:

K71	Second book published in 1967
K79	Tenth book published in 1967
K710	11th book published in 1967
K711	12th book published in 1967
K711-1	First supplement to the above item
K711-1;1	Second copy of the above supplement
K711;9	Tenth copy of the 12th book published in 1967

K8.1	Volume one published in 1968
K8.1;1	Second copy of the above
K8.1:g	Criticism of volume one
K8.2	Volume two published in a subsequent year
15K8	A work in Sanskrit published in 1968
15w1K8	A work in Sanskrit in verse published in 1968

References

1. Ranganathan, S.R. *Prolegomena to Library Classification.* 3rd ed.; assisted by M.A. Gopinath. Bombay: Asia Publishing House, 1967; Sec. UE3
2. *Ibid.*, UE3
3. Srivastava, A.P. *Theory of Knowledge Classification in Libraries.* New Delhi: Lakshmi Book Store, 1964; p. 184
4. Satija, M.P. *An Epistle to Dean Shera on the Brevity of Notation in Colon Classification.* Amritsar: Rajat Book Corner, p. 52
5. Ranganathan, *op. cit.*, Sec. UD 11
6. Comaromi, John P. *Book Numbers.* Littleton, Colo.: Libraries Unlimited, 1981; p. 46
7. Ranganathan, *op. cit.*, Sec. UE3
8. Ranganathan, S.R. *Colon Classification.* 6th ed. Bombay: Asia Publishing, 1963; Sec. 035 p. 1014
9. Ranganathan, *Prolegomena*, Sec. UA3
10. *Ibid.*, Sec. UE5

Further Reading

Satija, M.P. A Primer on Ranganathan's Book Number. Delhi: Mittal Publications, 1987. xvii, 87p.

This work explains Ranganathan's book number method in all its details, ramifications, and intricacies. The text has been illustrated with ample examples. "This is a simple and systematic exposition of the theory and practice of book numbers developed by Ranganathan" *Int. Classification* 15(2) 1988: 102.—Panline A Cochrane

Appendix 1

Isolates for Form Facet

a1	Systematical
a5	Alphabetical
a6	Chronological
b	Index
b1	Systematical
b5	Alphabetical
b51	Title
b55	Subject
b57	Author
c	List
c1	Systematical
c2	Numerical
c3	Geographical
c4	Conventional
c5	Alphabetical
c51	Title
c55	Subject
c57	Name
c6	Chronological
c9	Other types
c94	Printer
c96	Publisher
d	Data book
d2	Pattern
d3	Recipe
f	Picture
f2	Sculpture
f3	Engraving
f4	Graphic art
f5	Painting
f95	Photograph
f953	Cinema film
f9533	Sound film
f954	Negative
f955	Transparent picture
f994	Block
g	Plan
g1	Section
g2	Elevation
g3	Relief
g6	Diagram
h	Graph
h1	Line
h2	Histogram
h3	Perspective
h6	Schematic
j	Parody
k	Adaptation
m	Catechism
n	Opinion
p1	Lecture
p2	Dialogue
p3	Discussion
p5	Debate
p7	Symposium
q	Code
v	Practical
w1	Verse
w2	Drama
w3	Fiction
w4	Letter
w7	Champu
x	Quotation
x4	Press cutting.

Appendix 2

Language Facet Isolates

1	Indo-European	1517	Magdhi
11	Teutonic	1518	Anabhnomse
11011	Gothic	15198	Sinhalese
110153	Low Frisian	152	Hindi
110155	Old Frisian	153	Panjabi
111	English	154	Kashmiri
112	Dutch	155	Marathi
113	German	156	Gujarati
114	Swedish	157	Bengali
115	Norwegian	158	Assamese
116	Danish	1591	Oriya
117	Icelandic	1595	Nepali
12	Latin	16	Iranian
121	Italian	161	Avestic
122	French	162	Pahlavi
123	Spanish	164	Persian
124	Portuguese	165	Afghan (Pushtu)
128	Celtic	168	Urdu
1283	Welsh	17	Armenian
1285	Scotch, Gaelic	18	Albanian
13	Greek	191	Tocharish
14	Slavonic	192	Phyrigian
141	Lethic	197	Hittite
142	Russian	2	Semitic
143	Bulgarian	21	Babylonian including Syriac
144	Illyrian		
1441	Slav	22	Assyrian
1442	Serbian	24	Aramaic
145	Polish	25	Hebrew
146	Bohemian	26	Phoenician
15	Sanskrit	28	Arabic
151	Prakrit	3	Dravidian
1511	Pali	31	Tamil
1512	Maharastri	32	Malayalam
1516	Ardhamagadhi	33	Kanarese

34	Tulu	6	Other African languages
35	Telugu	7	Other American languages
36	Kui	8	Other Australian languages
38	Brahui	9	Other Oceanic languages
39	Toda, etc		Division 4-9 to be divided by (GD)
4	Other Asian Languages		
5	Other European languages		

Appendix 3

Isolate in (T): Chronological Division

A	Before 9999 B C	L	1700 to 1799 A D
A1	Eozoic	M	1800 to 1899 A D
A2	Palaeozoic	N	1900 to 1999 A D
A3	Mesozoic	P	2000 to 2099 A D
A4	Cenozoic	Q	2100 to 2199 A D
A5	Quaternary	R	2200 to 2299 A D
B	9999 to 1000 B C	S	2300 to 2399 A D
C	999 to 1 B C	T	2400 to 2499 A D
D	1 to 999 A D	U	2500 to 2599 A D
E	1000 to 1099 A D	V	2600 to 2699 A D
F	1100 to 1199 AD	W	2700 to 2799 A D
G	1200 to 1299 A D	X	2800 to 2899 A D
H	1300 to 1399 A D	YA	2900 to 2999 A D
I	1400 to 1499 A D	YB	3000 to 3099 A D
J	1500 to 1599 A D	YC	3100 to 3199 A D
K	1600 to 1699 A D		

CHAPTER 8

Rider Book Numbers

Fremont A. Rider (1885-1962) produced a purely enumerative and broad classification in an era that demanded minutely dilineated classes for any general scheme. His system, The Rider's International Classification, looms large as it sits on many a library science library shelf, but has not induced any use of it and little study on it.

Rider introduced his scheme of book numbers as an adjunct to his classification. He did not invent any thing new in it, but he did make things worse by his modifications. He proposed to use the Biscoe date table up to the decade, rather than to the year itself. So before we give examples of his misbegotten scheme we should give the Biscoe date table for ease of reference as the reader attempts to follow our exposition:

A	BC era	N	1870-1879
B	AD 1-999	O	1880-1889
C	1000-1499	P	1890-1899
D	1500-1599	Q	1900-1909
E	1600-1699	R	1910-1919
F	1700-1799	S	1920-1929
G	1800-1809	T	1930-1939
H	1810-1819	U	1940-1949
I	1820-1829	V	1950-1959
J	1830-1839	W	1960-1969
K	1840-1849	X	1970-1979
L	1850-1859	Y	1980-1989
M	1860-1869	Z	1990-1999

Thus, a book published in the year 1960 will receive the book number W. And *all* books published between 1960 and 1969 will receive W! It is more than likely that many books will be published on a specific subject within the same decade. We must have a means to individualize them. Rider chose as his individualizing element the access point of the main entry (usually the author's surname, but it could very well be the title of the work or the name of a corporate body). For example:

Mills: *Library Classification*, 1962 AHR WM

Here the W stands for the 1960s, the M for Mills.

Palmer: *Itself an Education*, 1962 AHR WP

Here the W stands for the 1960s and the P for Palmer. (The reader may wonder at such an odd title that Palmer concocted. From an early edition through the thirteenth, Melvil Dewey placed above the title of the DDC on the title page the motto: "To learn to classify is itself an education," written in one of Alexander Bains works on logic that Dewey surely was familiar with. "Classify" here means not to classify books using some general classification schedule, but rather to *make the classification schedule itself*. The reader must appreciate the difference.) If the author publishes more than two books on the same subject within the same decade, they are likely to get the same core book number. For example:

Ranganathan: *Elements of Library Classification*, 1962
Ranganathan: *Prolegomena to Library Classification*, 1967

2;5 and 2;5
WR WR

These are further individualized according to Rider's method by adding a, b, c, etc. The above two call numbers then become:

2;5 2;5
WR WRa

We have here a device to bring together all the books of the same author, for the same decade, of course.

For other complications including the problem of BC time, all the instructions meant for Biscoe numbers, are applicable here. Some of the objections raised with the Biscoe time number remain. On the other hand, it loses some of the advantages of the chronological book number, such as a decade is too long a span of time to study the development of a subject. It does not have much use, this classification of Rider, and can only be explained as a mindless effort of a man who tried to do too many things.

References

Rider, Fremont A. *Rider's International Classification for the Arrangement of Books on the Shelves of General Libraries*. Middletn, Conn.: The author, 1961

Young, Arthur P. "Rider, Arthur Fremont (1885-1962). *In ALA World Encyclopedia of Library and Information Science*, edited by Robert Wedgeworth. Chicago: ALA, 1986; pp. 709-710

CHAPTER 9

Merrill's Book Numbers

William Stetson Merill was born on January 16, 1866, in Newton, Massachusetts—less than a year after the American Civil War. He died on April 4, 1969, at 103—more than a year after the Tet Offensive of the Vietnam War. He graduated from Harvard in 1888 and went to work at the Newberry Library of Chicago under William F. Poole (of Poole's Index fame). When Poole died in 1895, Merrill became the head of the Classification Department. He decided to replace the broad classification preferred by Poole with the Expansive Classification of Cutter. The reclassification and the use of the EC caused so much difficulty for classifiers that Merrill felt obliged to offer in 1912 a course of lectures to assist them. The lectures were circulated in unpublished form for years. They were published by the American Library Association in 1928—the same year that they were translafed into Japanese by Shuko Kato—and again in 1939 and 1954. Its lastng value over those years is obvious. Its use would be with any classification; however, examples were given primarily for the Dewey Decimal Classification and the Library of Congress Classification. Since 1958, unfortunately, DDC principles have diverged considerably from Merrill's *Code for Classifiers*—to such an extent, in fact, that the Code would now mislead to an unacceptable degree. That is a shame because what Merrill set down was correct (and still is for LCC); it is the DDC practice that is no longer correct.

In 1912 Merrill brought before the eyes of the library world his book numbering scheme, published in an article in *Public Libraries* (April, 1912, pp. 127-129). His book numbers and his explanation of them follow:

The Merrill Book Numbers as explained by W.S. Merril himself.

The following tables of decimal numbers, hereby entirely printed have been in constant use at the Newberry library. The first table has been used also at the Library of Congress, the John Crerar library, and elsewhere for alphabeting names and headings; it was printed by Mr. James Duff Brown in his Subject classification (1906).

The three tables were designed respectively for names, periodical titles and dates. The numbers are to be treated as decimals and may be expanded by merely affixing additional figures without decimal point. They differ from the Cutter Alfabetic-order table numbers in employing only a numerical symbol without the initial letter of the name. To compare the example given in Table I: Bancroft is 07 in this table and B 22 in Mr Cutter's; Chicago is 16 in Merrill's and C 43 in his; History is 40 (or 4) in Merrill's and H 62 in his; Brockton is (by expansion) 123 in Merrill's and B 78 in his. Names intervening between two numbers are assigned the first number; when both numbers have been used, the first is expanded by merely affixing figures. For the sake of brevity it is well to leave gaps (e.g., to use 12, 122, 124) thus allowing for later insertions without the use of four figures. In crowded sections the numbers may be selected somewhat freely; in the case of long class-numbers the first figure only may be used.

Table II, for alphabeting titles of periodicals, is based upon the British Museum catalog of periodical publications and thus "fits the literature" better than the name table.

Table III furnishes a series of date abbreviations covering periods both before and after Christ in one sequence of numbers. For most purposes the decades before Christ are sufficiently minute subdivisions; if exact dates are desired, however, directions are given for constructing them.

The alternative figures at the right of the table employ one more figure than the other symbols; the symbols for dates after 1,000 are nothing but the dates themselves treated as decimal numbers, so that no symbol is necessary for exact dates.

The Cutter and Merrill numbers may be conveniently combined, if desired. For example, biographies of the same man written by different authors may be distinguished by affixing the Merrill number to the Cutter number, thus: Tarbell's life of Lincoln may be numbered L 6385—L 63 being the Cutter number for Lincoln and 85 the Merrill number for Tarbell. Again in literature, dates of works may be affixed to Cutter author number, e.g., M 6489 for Milton's Poetical works, 1890.

Copies of the following tables mounted upon cardboard for desk use then could be obtained from the author, care of the Newberry Library, Chicago, III.

WILLIM STETSON MERRILL.

Merrill numbers

TABLE 1.
PERSONS—PLACES—THINGS.

The decimal numbers given in Table I are designed for alphabeting names of persons, places, titles or things, e.g.:

Bancroft	....	07
Chicago	....	16
History	....	40
Coffee	....	18

Additional numbers may be formed by merely affixing figures, e.g.:

Brimfield	....	12
Brockton	....	123
Brookline	....	127

Shorter numbers may be obtained by dropping the second figure, e.g.:

History	....	4
London	....	5

01	A	17	Ci
02	Agr	18	Clo
03	Als	19	Cond
04	Ap	20	Crom
05	Ash	21	D
06	B	22	Day
07	Ban	23	Dick
08	Bax	24	Doy
09	Beno	25	E
10	Bix	26	Elg
11	Bou	27	Erm
12	Brim	28	F
13	Bum	29	Fel
14	C	30	Fit
15	Carr	31	Forr
16	Chan	32	G

33	Gay
34	Gill
35	Goe
36	Got
37	Greene
38	H
39	Hat
40	Hesi
41	Hiu
42	Hov
43	I
44	Ini
45	J
46	K
47	L
48	Lang
49	Law
50	Leo
51	Lit
52	Long
53	M
54	McL
55	Marc
56	Mau
57	Merr
58	Min
59	Moo
60	Mu
61	N
62	Nev
63	Nol
64	O
65	P
66	Park
67	Pek
68	Pfi
69	Pif
70	Po
71	Pow
72	Q
73	R
74	Ray
75	Robi
76	Row
77	S
78	Sanc
79	Scha
80	Schw
81	Sevi
82	Simon
83	Soo
84	Steb
85	Strat
86	T
87	Thau
88	To
89	Trum
90	U
91	Ull
92	Upt
93	V
94	Ven
95	W
96	Wats
97	Wha
98	Wit
99	W-Z

TABLE II.
PERIODICAL TITLES.

01	Aa	Alman
02	Albu	Amerid

05 Annales
06 Annual
07 Annuar
08 Archiv
09 Arçhives
10 Ast
11 B
12 Bell
13 Bibliot
14 Blat
15 Blow
16 British
17 Bulletin
18 Camd
19 Cent
20 Chili
21 Christl
22 Civ
23 Comm
24 Corn
25 Cra
26 Danz
27 Deutsche
28 Dra
29 Ech
30 Elo
31 Esp
32 Exh
33 Fish
34 Freed
35 Gaz
36 Geni
37 Gla
38 Gri
39 Hap
40 Historic
41 I
42 Int
43 J
44 Jahre
45 Journal
46 Journal di
47 Journal p
48 K
49 Kos
50 Lav
51 Libu
52 Literary
53 London
54 Magazine
55 Magb
56 Math
57 Memo
58 Mid
59 Mitt
60 Monthly
61 Monti
62 Musi
63 N
64 Neu
65 Nev
66 New
67 North
68 Nuo
69 Og
70 Osw
71 Pari
72 Peo
73 Phr
74 Poln
75 Pres
76 Ps
77 R
78 Ret
79 Repu
80 Revue
81 Rey
82 Roy
83 Salm
84 Schm

85	Sem
86	Sl
87	Stad
88	Su
89	T
90	The
91	Tim
92	Tro
93	V
94	W
95	Wel
96	Wo
97	Zeitg
98	Zeitschrift
99	Zeitst

FRENCH PERIODICALS

REVUE

a-c	.8
de	.801
de s	.802
du a	.803
du c	.804
du e	.805
du g	.806
du j	.807
du m	.808
du r	.809

TABLE III.

TIME DECIMALS.

(Explanation.)

The following two-figure date numbers cover years before and after Christ in one series. The two figures given at the left of the dates stand for decades since 1500 A.D., and for centuries before 1500.

The precise year after 1500 may be designated by dropping the first figure of the date, e.g.: 522=1522 A.D.; 688=1688 A.D.; 911=1911 A.D.

The precise year between 1 and 1500 A.D. may be designated by affixing the last two figures of the date to the number for the century, e.g.: 4492=1492 A.D.; 4066=1066 A.D.; 3325=325 A.D.

Numbers for exact dates B.C. may be formed by taking the number for the century and affixing the following substitutes for the last two figures of the date: 9 for 1, 8 for 2, 7 for 3, 6 for 4, 5 for 5, 4 for 6, 3 for 7, 2 for 8, 1 for 9, e.g.:
1787=323 B.C. i.e. 17=4th century; 8=2; 7=3. 2066=44 B.C. i.e. 20=1st century; 6=4; 6=4.

The alternative numbers given at the right are longer but avoid the transition from figures to letters with the advent of the year 2000 A.D. For exact years after 1500 use whole date; e.g. 1522, 1775.

TABLE III.
TIME DECIMALS.

NOTE—For convenience of expanding the numbers the last year of each century or decade appears under the section following: e.g. 1800 appear under 19th century.

		Alternative
0	PREHISTORIC	
1	ANTIQUITY	0
11	Before 900 B.C.	
12	899—800 B.C.	9th c. 00
13	799—700 B.C.	8th c. 01
14	699—600 B.C.	7th c. 02
15	599—500 B.C.	6th c. 03
16	499—400 B.C.	5th c. 04
17	399—300 B.C.	4th c. 05
18	299—200 B.C.	3d c. 06
19	199—100 B.C.	2d c. 07
20	99— 1 B.C.	1st c. 08
3	CHRISTIAN ERA	09
30	0— 99 A.D.	1st c. 090
31	100—199 A.D.	2d c. 091
32	200—299 A.D.	3d c. 092
33	300—399 A.D.	4th c. 093
34	400—499 A.D.	5th c. 094
35	500—599 A.D.	6th c. 095
36	600—699 A.D.	7th c. 096
37	700—799 A.D.	8th c. 097
38	800—899 A.D.	9th c. 098
39	900—999 A.D.	10th c. 099
4	MIDDLE AGES	1
40	1000—1099 A.D.	11th c. 10
41	1100—1199 A.D.	12th c. 11
42	1200—1299 A.D.	13th c. 12
43	1300—1399 A.D.	14th c. 13
44	1400—1499 A.D.	15th c. 14

5	SIXTEENTH CENTURY	15
50	1500—1509	150
51	1510—1519	151
52	1520—1529	152
53	1530—1539	153
54	1540—1549	154
55	1550—1559	155
56	1560—1569	156
57	1570—1579	157
58	1580—1589	158
59	1590—1599	159
6	SEVENTEENTH CENTURY	16
60	1600—1609	160
61	1610—1619	161
62	1620—1629	162
63	1630—1639	163
64	1640—1649	164
65	1650—1659	165
66	1660—1669	166
67	1670—1679	167
68	1680—1689	168
69	1690—1699	169
7	EIGHTEENTH CENTURY	17
70	1700—1709	170
71	1710—1719	171
72	1720—1729	172
73	1730—1739	173
74	1470—1749	174
75	1750—1759	175
76	1770—1779	176
77	1770—1779	177
78	1780—1789	178
79	1790—1799	179
8	NINETEENTH CENTURY	18
80	1800—1809	180
81	1810—1819	181
82	1820—1829	182

83	1830—1839	183
84	1840—1859	184
85	1580—1859	185
86	1860—1869	186
87	1870—1879	187
88	1880—1889	188
89	1890—1899	189
9	TWENTIETH CENTURY	19
90	1900—1909	190
91	1910—1919	191
92	1920—1929	192
93	1930—1939	193

etc.

A0	TWENTY—FIRST CENTURY	2
A 00	2000—2009	20
A 01	2010—2019	201
A 02	2020—2029	202
A 03	2030—2039	203

etc.

Table 1 (mentioned earlier) is simple too blad to be of much value in a large library. We are surprised that Merrill would propose it for use anywhere, let alone in a great library like the Newberry. Table 2 (for periodicals) is well founded inasmuch as it is based on the periodicals list of the British Museum. Its practicality can be seen in the special development for French reveues.

Table 3 is clever, well-designed, and the most extensive of all date tables as far as extension into the future is concerned: The future is more likely to run out than Merrill's numbers for it. Its serious flaw, however, is that not until the 21st century will letters be a part of the number. Free-floating Arabic numerals tend to be ambiguous, misunderstod, and attached to the class number (an especial danger with respect to the DDC)-for which reasons Merrill's Table 3 book numbers were never widely accepted. his Table 1 and 2 book numbers had not much more success.

Appendices

A Chronology of Book Numbers

1873 Melvil Dewey devised the first fully relative classification and applied it to the Amherst College Library (Massachusetts). Further sub-arrangement within a given class was by author spelled in full or brief. Alphabetical sub-arrangement was soon replaced by an accession method in which integers were attached to class numbers to indicate the order in which a particular work arrived in a given class. The number provided both the size of the class and the currency of the work (when it was not published previously).

1876 Melvil Dewey published his scheme for the arrangement of library books and lesser pieces of writing (e.g., articles, segments of encyclopedias). He created a revolution in the development of library classification.

1878 Cutter proposed that it is necessary to set apart the book number from the class number. He also suggested that author numbers should be decimal fractions so as to permit further expansion and interpolation wherever necessary. It was a major breakthrough. He also published a table of number to effect his ideas.

1879 A symposium on book numbers was published in Library Journal wherein leading librarians, primarily Melvil Dewey, C.A. Cutter, J.N. Larned, John Edmands, F.B. Perkins, and John Fitzpatrick contributed. John Edmands, librarian of the Philadelphia Mercantile Library, proposed a plan to use the initial letter of the author's surname followed by decimal digits to represent the rest of the other letters of the name. (It is Comaromi's view that Edmands' idea was the beginning of author numbers as we know them.) The symposium proved to be a milestone in the development of book numbers.

1880 Cutter printed a preliminary version of his two-figure author table and made it available commercially. No copies appear to have survived.

1885 Walter Stanley Biscoe, Dewey's subaltern and friend then at Columbia College with him, proposed a chronological book number system, which suggested a path different from that of the author arrangement prevalent at that time.

1886 Cutter published a special table for Latin and Greek authors in which a sub-arrangement for works by and about a particular author was presented. It was done on the lines of the Shakespeare table that he had done earlier, though more developed.

1886 At the American Library Association annual conference for 1886 that was held in Milwaukee, Wisconsin, Dewey spoke of eclectic book numbers, and presented some basic ideas on book numbers. Lehnus concluded that the discussion at the conference was the most complete discussion of the various methods of sub-arranging books that ever appeared in the literature.

1886 Cutters *Alfabetic order Table* was published. It was a revised table of his 1880 table.

1888 Cutter revised and reprinted his two-figure table.

1888 During the ALA conference there was a symposium on the use of Cutter numbers in connection with the DDC. Many librarians, including Cutter, participated in the discussions on the use and problems of book numbers.

1893 C.R. Olin of Buchtel College (now the University of Akron) devised an alphabetical table to be used for arranging collective biographies.

1892 Cutter made arrangement with a former assistant at the Boston Athenaeum, Miss Kate Emery Sanborn, then cataloger at the St. Louis Mercantile Library, to expand his table to three figures to meet the demand of the larger or growing libraries. The first revision by Sanborn, published in 1892, was for S and the vowels.

1895 The Sanborn revision for the remaining twenty letters was published.

1896 The two tables by Sanborn were combined and printed as a single table by the Library Bureau of Boston. This three-figure author table was incompatible with Cutter's two-figure author table. Libraries using the earlier Cutter table could not use the Cutter-Sanborn table.

1898 The Library of Congress began using Cutter numbers for part of the Library of Congress Classification (primarily for literature).

1899 Aghast at Sanborn's expansion, Cutter announced a true expansion of his two-figure table.

1901-1902 Cutter's three-figure table is completed and made available. In vain, Cutter hoped that this new table would replace the Sanborn revision, already entrenched in American libraries.

1902 The Library of Congress published its book numbering procedures based on one or other of the Cutter author tables (including the Cutter-Sanborn author table).

1906 James Duff Brown proposed his chronological book number system in his subject Classification.

1912 S.D. Jast published his alphabetical book numbers.

1912 William Stetson Merrill published his Merrill author-table.

1917 Anna Cantrell Laws' *Author Notation in the Library of Congress* published.

1933 Ranganathan's chronological book numbers published as a part of his Colon Classification.

1937 Bertha Rickenrode Barden brought out her *Book Numbers: a Manual for Students with a Basic Code of Rules.*

1961 Fremont A. Rider proposed a modification of the Biscoe date table in his International Classification.

1969 All Cutter tables (the Cutter two-figure table, the Cutter three-figure table, and the Cutter-Sanborn three-figure author table) were revised. They were corrected and published in the Swanson-Swift revisions and distributed by the H.R. Huntting Company of Chicopee, Massachusetts, early on, but then by Libraries Unlimited, Englewood, Colorado, with the permission of Richard Charles Cutter. The revisions were edited by Paul K. Swanson and Esther M. Swift.

1971 Anna C. Laws' book (1937) reprinted.

1980 Donald J. Lehnus's *Book Numbers: History, Principles, and Applications* published.

1981 John P. Comaromi's *Book Numbers: a Historical Study and Practical Guide to Their Use* published.

1987 Mohinder Partap Satija's *A Primer on Ranganathan's Book Numbers* published.

1990 *Encyclopedia of Library and Information Science,* edited by A. Kent. Vol. 45 (1990) contains a long article on book and call numbers by M.P. Satija.

1990 M.P. Satija and S.P. Agarwal, *Book Numbers: Some Indian Methods.* New Delhi: Concept Publishing, published.

1991 Karen M Drabenstott discussed the designing of an expert system for shelflisting at the 5th International Study Conference in Classification Research held Toronto, June 1991.

Bibliography

The main sources of a bibliography on book numbers are the books by Miss Barden (1937), Lehnus (1980) and Comaromi (1981) and the article on Book number in *Encyclopaedia of Library & Information Science*, edited by Allen Kent, Vol. 45 (Marcel Dekker, 1990). Of these, Lehnus is especially important for this purpose as it gives a bibliography of 67 items given in chronological order. Though the largest bibliography ever compiled on the subject it only confines to American writings on the subject from 1876 to 1978 (Book numbers has essentially remained as American subject. It sprouted and developed on Amrican soil). So far all the major books published are all American. In addition to these, some earlier textbooks such as by Margaret Mann (1930) and Susan Grey Akers (1933) also yield some good references. The bibliography on classification by Barbara Denison: *Selected material on classification* (New york: Special Library Association, 1968) has some references on book numbers mostly pertaining to the local practices followed in the United State libraries. Another such source is I. Dahlberg's *International Classification and Indexing Bibliography*. Frankfurt: Indeks Verlag, 1985, Vol. 3 p 80-81). It has about a dozen references including some published in Europeans languages (especially German) from 1950 onwards.

Book numbers is perhaps a closed topic now; that is why there is not much literature coming forth presently. Books by Lehnus and Comaromi are a sort of surprise; or should we say that these are renewed efforts to revive the subject. One result is the book in hand.

Most of the literature available on book numbers falls into the following categories:
(1) Author tables and other specific and special book numbering methods. Most of this kind of literature pertains to 19th century and early twentieth century.
(2) General and theoretical introduction to book numbers; their nature and purpose. Such a literature is mostly embodied in textbooks.
(3) Explanation and exposition of a particular book numbering system. Most of this type of literature is in classification textbooks published in India; and these mostly rehash Ranganathan's book number.

This bibliography aims to garner references of all such types, and subsumes entries in all other bibliographies on book numbers. This bibliography almost exhaustive of the entire Indian and American literature of the subject is now the largest but succinct bibliography ever compiled on the topic. Hope it is exhaustive of the literature published in English. Efforts have not been spared even to trace hidden and explicit references on the subject published in Europe. Yet it lays no claim on exhaustivity for the simple reason that many more local practices and the author tables designed for non-English languages are not reported in the literature especially the LIS literature in English.

The arrangement of entries is by the year of publication. Within a given year, the arrangement is by author - or by title if there is no author. Further arrangement, if needed, is by title. Every entry contains full bibliographical description and some of them are annotated. Non-English references have been marked with an asterisk. Author, Index to the bibliography immediately follows it:

1878

1 1) Cutter, C.A.: "Another plan for numbering books". *Lib Jl* 3 (Sept 1878): 248-251.

2 2) Schwartz, Jacob: "A 'combined' system for arranging and numbering". *Lib jl* 3 (March 1978): 6-10.

3 3) Schwartz, Jacob: "Mr Cutter's numbering Plan". *Lib jl* 3 (Oct. 1978): 302.

1879

4 1) Dewey, Melvil: "Arrangment on the shelves - first paper". *Lib Jl* 4 (April 1979): 117-120.

5 2) Dewey, Melvil: "Arrangement on the shelves - second paper". *Lib Jl* 4 (June 1879): 191-194.

6 3) Dewey, Melvil: "Principles underlying numbering systems - second paper: a new numbering base". *Lib jl* 4 (Mar 1879): 75-79.

7 4) Dewey, Melvil: "Principles underlying numbering systems - first paper". *Lib Jl* 4 (Jan 1879): 7-10.

8 5) Edmands, John: "Proportion of initial letters in author catalogs". *Lib Jl* (Feb 1879): 56.

9 6) "Plans for numbering, with special reference to fiction: a library symposium". *Lib Jl* 4 (Feb 1879): 38-47. Contribution by John Edmands, Josephus N Larned, M. Dewey, C.A. Cutter and Frederick B Perkins.

1880

10 1) Cutter's decimal author table. Boston, 1880. The first Commercially sold table by Cutter. This table is now non-extant.

1881

11 1) Massey, A.P. "Classification of fiction". *Lib Jl* 6 (Jan 1881): 7-9.

1882

12 1) Cutter, C.A.: *Boston Athenaeum: How to get books, with an explanation of the new way of marking books.* Boston: Press of Rockwell and Churchill, 1882. pp. 14-18, 35-36.

13 2) Fitzgerald, John: "Mnemonic numbering". *Lib Jl* 7 (Sept 1882): 229-230.

14 3) Schwartz, Jacob: "A new classification and notation". *Lib Jl* 7 (July-Aug 1882): 148-166.

1884

15 1) Cutter, C.A.: "Arrangement and notation for Shakespeariana". *Lib Jl* 9 (Aug 1884): 139-139.

16 2) Lane, William Coolidge. Plan adopted for Greek and Latin authors. *Lib Jl* 9 (March 1884): 50-51.

1885

17 1) Biscoe, Walter Stanley: "Chronological arrangement on shelves". *Lib Jl* 10 (Sept-Oct 1885): 245-246.

18 2) Goddard, E.N.: "Classification of fiction". *Lib Jl* 10 (Mar 1885): 55.

19 3) Lane, William Coolidge: "Report on classification, 1883-85". *Lib Jl* 10 (Sept-Oct 1885): 257-261.

1886

20 1) Cutter's Alfabetic-order table. Boston: 1886. 2pp. 28x28 cm.

21 2) Cutter, C.A.: "Author-table for Greek and Latin authors". *Lib Jl* 11 (Aug-Sept 1886): 280-289.

22 3) Dewey, Melvil: "Eclectic book-numers". *Lib Jl* 11 (Aug-Sept 1886): 296-301.

23 4) Swan, Charles H: "Alfab-order table for names of places". *Lib Jl* 11 (Apr 1886): 118.

1887

24 1) Cole, George Watson: "Some thoughts on close classification". *Lib Jl* 12 (Sept-Oct 1887): 360.

25 2) Cutter, C.A.: "Cutter's author-table: the arrangement of biography". *Lib Jl* 12 (Dec 1887) 544.

26 3) Cutter, C.A.: "How to use Cutter's decimal author table". *Lib Jl* 12 (July 1887): 251-252 and (Dec 1887): 549.

27 4) "Libraries on special authors". *Lib Notes* 2 (June 1887): 14-16.

1888

28 1) "Cutter author-numbers in connection with the Dewey Classification: a symposium" *Lib Jl* 13 (Sept-Oct 1888): 308-309.

29 2) Cutter, C.A.: "Adversaria" *Lib Jl* 13 (Mar-April 1888): 79

30 3) Cutter, C.A.: Alfabetic-order table. Rev ed. Boston, 1888. 4pp. 31x31 cm.

1891

31 1) Cutter, C.A.: "The Cutter author marks: why and how they are used". In his: *Expansive Classification:* sixth expansion. Pt. I Boston: The Author, 1891-1893. pp. 139-160. This also includes his author table for Greek and Latin authors, which was also published as a separate pamphlet.

1892

32 1) C.A. Cutter's alfabetic order table. Alternatives for the vowels and S (Single initials to be used instead of the first two letters) by Miss Kate E Sanborn. Boston: Library Bureau, 1892. 4pp. 33x17 cm.

1893

33 1) "Book numbers". *Lib Notes* 3 (Oct 1893): 419-450. A special issue on book numbers. Discusses definition, principles, special book number schemes for library books and for special and prolific writers. Also discusses chronological book number of W S Biscoe.

Melvil Dewey began *Library Notes* to advance his ideas, no doubt to sell products that he sponsored or approved volumes (1886-1898) are a mirror to the library practice of the period. This is a special issue on book numbers that discusses such things as the definition of book numbers, their principles, special book number schemes discussion of chronological book numbers.

34 2) Olin, C.R.: "An order table for collective biography". *Lib Jl* 18 (May 1893): 144.

35 3) Richardson, Ernest Cushing. "An expansve author-table". *Lib Jl* 18 (June 1893): 187.

1895

36 1) C.A. Cutter's alfabetic-order table - consonants, except S. Altered and fitted with three letters by Miss Kate E Sanborn. Boston: Library Bureau, 1895. 14p. 33x28 cm.
It is independent of Cutter's two figure author table.
It is widely used in the English speaking world.

1896.

37 1) C.A. Cutter's alfabetic-order table - consonants, except S and vowels and S. Altered and fitted with three figures by Miss Kate E Sanborn. Boston: Library Bureau, 1896. 18pp. 33x19 cm.
We enter the work under Cutter for the sake of convenience rather than accuracy. The work is, in fact, original with Sanborn and quite independent of Cutter's two-figure author table. This is the author table that is most widely used in the English-speaking world. When a Cutter table is spoken of, this is the one that is meant.

38 2) Cutter, C.A.: "Comment" *Lib Jl* 21 (Oct 1896): 443

39 3) Langton, H.H.: "Systems of shelf-notation". *Lib Jl* 21 (Oct 1896): 441-443.

1898

40 1) Dewey, Melvil. *Simplified library school rules: card catalog, accession, book numbers, shelf list, capitals, punctuations, abbreviations, library handwriting*. Boston, N.Y.: Library Bureau, 1898. Book Numbers, pp. 53-60.

41 2) Windeyer, Margaret: "The Cutter book numbers". *Proceedings of the Sydney Meeting of the Library Association of Australasia, October, 1898*. Sydney: Hennessey, Campbell & Co, 1898, pp. 30-31.

1899

42 1) Cutter, C.A.: Explanation of the Cutter-Sanborn authormaks (three-figure tables). 3rd ed. Northampton, Mass: Herald Office, 1899.

1901

43 1) Anderson, P.J.: "Author and work marks" A letter to the Editor *The Library World* 3(35) May 1901: 279-280.

44 2) Ashley, Frederick W: "Size marks for class numbers". *Lib Jl* 26 (Jan 1901): 22.

45 3) C.A. Cutter's three-figure alfabetic-order table-consonants except S and vowels and S. Boston: Library Bureau, 1901. 26pp. 34x19 cm.

46 4) Cutter, C.A.: *Explanation of the alphabetic-order marks* (three-figure tables). Northampton, Mass: C.A. Pierce & Co, 1901.

1902

47 1) Daniels, Joseph F: "Author and title marks in fiction". *Pub Libraries* 7 (April 1902): 143-144.

48 2) Library of Congress. Shelf list rules. Washington: Government Printing Office, 1902.

1904

49 1) Cutter, C.A.: Explanation of the Cutter-Sanborn authormarks (three-figure tables). 4th ed. rev. by Kate Emery Sanborn. Boston: Library bureau, 1904.

1906

50 1) Brown, James Duff: "Notation - the numbering of books". In his: *Subject classification.* London: The Library Supply Co, 1906, pp. 26-33.

1910

51 1) Bliss, H.E.: "Simplified book-notation". *Lib Jl* 35 (Dec 1910): 544-546.

1911

52 1) Cutter, Charles Ammi: Explanation of the alphabetic order marks (two figure tables). Northampton, Mass: Herald Job Print, 1911.

53 2) Mead, H. Ralph: "Some problems in book numbers". *ALA Bulletin* 5 (May-July 1911): 251-253.

1912

54 1) Bliss, H.E.: "A simplified alphabetic order table". *Lib Jl* 37 (Feb 1912): 71-74.

55 2) Jast, S.D.: "Book numbers". *Lib World* 3 (1912): 120-123; 150-152.

56 3) Merrill, William Stetson. "The Merrill book numbers". *Public libraries* 17 (April 1912): 127-129.

1914

57 1) Brown, James Duff. *Subject classification* 2nd ed. London: Grafton, 1914. pp. 26-32.

1916

58 1) Dickinson, Asa Don: *Punjab library primer*.Lahore: University of the Punjab, 1916, 242p. In this especially written manual to suit Indian libraries a simple two-figure author table has been given.

1917

59 1) Andrews, C.W.: "Principles of classification". *ALA Bulletin* 11 (July 1917): 195-197.

60 2) Fletcher, William Isaac: "Some notes on classification". *ALA Bulletin* 11 (July 1917): 340-341.

61 3) Laws, Anna Cantrell: *Author notation in the Library of Congress*. Washington: Government printing Office, 1917, 18p. States the book numbering policy and procedure of the Processing Division of the US Library of Congress. It is a source book and of immense historical value. This is a sourcebook of enormous historical value. It gives the book number policy and procedure of the Processing Division of the Library of Congress.

62 4) Merrill, W.S.: "Merrill book numbers". *Public Libraries* 17 (April 1917): 127-129.

1919

63 1) Wiley, Edwin. "Some sidelights on classification". *Lib Jl* 44 (June 1919): 363.

64 2) University of Chicago Library. *Rules for shelflisting*. Chicago: University of Chicago Press, 1919.

1924

65 1) Dewey, Melvil, "Temporary fads". *Lib Jl* 49 (Jan 1, 1924): 38

1925

66 1) Bacon, Corinne: *Classification*. Rev. ed. Chicago: ALA, 1925, pp. 23-29, 37

1926

67 1) Parker, Henry William: *Library classification and numbering system*. 3rd ed. New York: Printed by JJ Little and Ives Co, 1926 203p.

68 2) Sayers, W.C.B.: *Manual of classification*. London: Grafton, 1926. pp. 231-235.

69 3) American Library Association. *Survey of libraries in the United States*. Chicago: ALA, 1926-1927, Vol. 4, pp. 15-17.

1930

70 1) Mann, Margaret: *Introduction to cataloguing and classification of books*. Chicago: ALA, 1920, pp. 114-126. Bibliography, pp. 131-132.

1932

71 1) Brown, Zaidee. "More about Cutter numbers". Lib Jl 57 (May 1, 1932): 437.

72 2) Dewey, Melvil: *Decimal classification and relative index*. 13th ed. edited by J. Dorcas Fellow and Myron W. Getchell. Albany, N.Y.: The Forest Press, 1932, pp. 1643-1644.

73 3) Tomlinson, Anna Louise: "Are Cutter number doomed"?. *Lib Jl* 57 (Mar 15, 1932): 292.

1933

74 1) Akers, Susan Grey: *Simple library cataloguing*. 2nd ed. Chicago: ALA, 1933, pp. 16-17.

75 2) Ranganathan, S.R.: *Colon classification*. Madras: The Madras Library Association, 1933. 3pts. Proposed a new system of chronological book numbers.

1937

76 1) Barden, Bertha R: *Book numbers: a manual for students with a basic code of rules*. Chicago: American Library Association, 1937, p31 (Reprinted 1971) A very useful guide and a classic name in book numbers. Besides a very brief history of book numbers gives some special schemes and a selected bibliography in the end (pp. 30-31).

77 2) Ranganathan, S.R.: "Book number' In his: *Prolegomena to library classification.* Madras: Madras Library Association, 1937, pp. 175-81.

1938

78 1) Bliss, H.E.: *Organization of knowledge in libraries.* New York: H.W. Wilson, 1938, p.68.

1939

79 1) Brown, James Duff: *Subject classification.* 3rd ed. rev. by J.D. Stewart. London: Grafton, 1939. pp. 27-32.

1940

80 1) Neiswanger, Laura. "Book numbers in University libraries" *Cataloguers and classifiers' year book,* No. 8, 1939. Chicago: American Library Association, 1940. pp. 88-95.
Gives some special schemes of book numbers as an improvement over Bertha Barden's suggestions.

1943

81 1) Mann, Margaret. *Introduction to cataloging and classificaton of books.* 2nd ed. Chicago: ALA, 1943. (1971 Reprint), pp. 86-94.

1947

82 1) Moore M, and Holleman, W.R.: "Cataloguing commerical material". *Spl libraries* 38 1947: 295-297. Describes a method of cataloguing of trade literature which has its bases in Cutter-Sanborn numbers for names of Commercial Companies. This table was developed at the Boeing Airplane Co library.

1950

83 1) Garde, P.K.: "Pseudo classics", *Annals of Ind. Lib. Asso.* 1, 1950: 15-19.

1951

84 1) Phillips, W. Howard. *A primer of book classification.* Rev. ed. London: Association of Assistant Librarians, 1951, pp. 53.

1952

85 1) Jesse, William Herman: *Shelf work in libraries.* Chicago: ALA, 1952, 68p.

1953

86 1) *Fuchs, W: *Sachliche ordnung, aufstellung and signature in ihrem rationellen verhaltnis: optimate notation in optimal geordnet aufgestellter bibliothek.* [Subject-oriented order, shelving and call numbers seen in an optimal arranged library]. *Zentralbl. f. Bibl wes* 67 (1953): 438-458.
In German language.

87 2) Ujlambkar, K.M.: "Form part of Ranganathan's book number". In: *Depth classification.* ed by S R Ranganathan. Delhi: ILA, 1953, p. 126

1954

88 1) Akers, Susan Grey: *Simple library cataloguing*, 4th ed. Chicago: ALA, 1954. Book Numbers, pp. 20-24.

89 2) *Alker, H: "Aufstellung and signaturen der universitats-bibliothek Wien" [Shelving and call numbers of the university library of Vienna]. *Zentralbl.f.Blbl wes.* 68 (1954): 241-252.
In German language.

90 3) *Zuber, Mohammed and Agrawal, S.P.: *Pustak-sankhya Prevashika.* [Introduction to book numbers] Aligarh: Shanker Prakashan, 1954, 52p. This booklet in Hindi language is a manual on assigning author numbers for English names as designed by Asa Don Dickinson, with modifications as suggested by professor S. Bashiruddin. Author Table for Roman alphabets is also given.

1955

91 1) *Gunzenhauser, M: Optimale signatur and zweckmassige Aufstellung der Bestande [Optimal call numbers and useful shelving of holdings]. *Zentralbl.f.Bibl. wes* 69 1955:356-363 In German language.

92 2) Mayol, Josefina: "Author numbers for Spanish names in the literature class". *Jl of Cataloging and classification.* 11 (July 1955): 138-143.

93 3) *Uhlmanna A: Bibliothekssignaturen [Library call numbers] Miskole, 1955. (A Rakasi Matyas Nehezipari Muszake Egyetem Konyvtaranak Kiadvanyai.3)
In Hungarian language.
As we are in the bibliography some license may be taken. One of the authors of the present work (Comaromi) takes his name from a Hungarian province-Komarom. He does so by virtue of a man, Michael Komaromy, who adopted six Austrian orphans, named Koch, for want of a better name. The orphans took the adoptive father's name. One of them subsequently married a Czech woman who demanded equal religious rights. That is, half their children were to have a Roman Catholic form of name (like Comaromi) and half a form that was more Orthodox (like Komaromy). We write this only to say that names do not depict origins necessarily and to warn the classifier that all things are not as they seem.

1956

94 1) *Hilgenberg, O.Ch: "Uber die signatur von Bibliotheksgut" [On the call numbers of library holdings] *Zentralbl f Bibl wes* 70 (1956): 174-203.
In German Language

1957

95 1) *Holock, J. "Om afskaffelse af forefattermaekes" [About the doing away with author numbers]. *Bibliotekaren* 19(1) 1957: 1-4.

96 2) Ranganathan, S.R.: "Book Numbers etc". In his: *Prolegomena* 2nd ed. London: LA, 1957, pp. 371-387.

1959

97 1) Ranganathan, S.R.: *Colon Classification.* 6th ed. Bombay: Asia Publish-

ing House, 1959. Book numbers. Chap. 03, pp. 109 to 1.17
98 2) Sayers, W.C.B.: "Book and work numbers". In his: *A Manual of classification and librarians and bibliographers*, 3rd rev. ed. London: Andre Deutsch, 1959, pp. 243-246.

1961
99 1) India. National Library: *Author table for Indian names*. Calcutta: National Library, 1961, viii, 255p.
100 2) Rider, Fremont A: *Rider's International classification for the arrangement of books on the shelves of general libraries*. Middleton, Conn: The Author, 1961. "Introduction" and pages 923-929.

1962
101 1) Chakrabarti, S.N.: "Some modern problems in assigning author numbers and book numbers in classifying books". *Indian Librarian* 17 (Sept 1962): 109-112.
102 2) *Malaga, Luis F: *Tables de notacion interna para bibliotecas hispanicas* (de dos y tres cifras), *Con un codigo de reglas para su aplication*. Washingtn: Union Panamericana, 1962.
In Spanish language.
103 3) Phillips, W.H.: *A primer of book classification*. London: Association of Assistant Librarians, 1962.

1963
104 1) Sarkar, D.C.: "Rendering of Indic names of persons for catalogue entry and shelf-arrangement - a neglected aspect". *Iaslic Bull* 8(3) Sept 1963: 116-123.

1964
105 1) Parkhi, R.S.: *Decimal classification and colon classification in perspective*. Bombay: Asia Publishing House, 1964. Book Numbers, pp. 507-520. Makes a comparative study of the book numbering method used in these two systems.
106 2) Srivastava, Anand P: *Theory of knowledge classification in libraries*. New Delhi: Lakshmi Book Store, 1964, pp. 169-186.
A chapter gives a very lucid account of the nature and purpose of book numbers with special reference to Ranganathan's system.

1965
107 1) Binwal, J.C. and Singh, Lal Mani Prasad: "Edition facet in book numbers". *Herald of lib sc.* 4(1) (Jan 1965): 66-71. Dwells upon the drawback of separation of different editions of a book in colon book number; and suggests some remedial measures.
108 2) *Gunzenhauser, M: "Optimale signatur und Zweckma Bige aufstellung der bestande" Optimal call numbers and useful shelving of holdings. *Zentralbl. f.Bibl. wes* 69 (1965): 356-363.
In German language.
109 3) Merryman, John Henry and Long, Rosalee M: "A new author Notation" *Library Resources and Technical Services* 9 (Summer 1965): 356-358.

1966

110 1) Batty, C.D.: *An introduction to colon classification*. London: Clive Bingley, 1966, p. 89

111 2) Gore, Daniel: Further observationson the use of LC classification". *Lib Res & Tech Serv* 10 Fall 1966: 519-524.
Suggests amendments in LC cuttering method.

112 3) Kumar, B.K: "Filing of entries for Chinese titles". *Herald of lib sc* 5(4) Oct 1966: 297-300.

113 4) Merryman, John Henry and Long, Rosalee M: *Author notation* Stanford Calif: Stanford Law Library, 1966, v, 142p.

114 5) Ranganathan, S.R.: "Facets of book number". In his: *Library Manual*. 2nd ed. Bombay: Asia Publishing House, 1966, pp. 341-343.
Gives Ranganathan's book number in brief for use in small libraries.

1967

115 1) Boyd, A.H.: "Computer processing of library of Congress book numbers". *Program* 4 1967: 1-7.
"Deals with problems associated with processing before book numbers can be sorted to obtain alphabetically and numerically ordered lists".

116 2) Ranganathan, S.R.: *Prolegomena to library classification*. 3rd ed, assisted by M.A. Gopinath. Bombay: Asia Publishing House, 1967, Pt U, pp. 501-510.
A brief account of various book numbering systems. Inevitably his own system has been dealt in detail.

117 3) Sayers, W.C.B.: *A manual of classification for librarians*. London: Andre Deutsch, 1967.

1968

118 1) Arick, N.C.: "Subclassification and book numbers of documents and official publications". In: *Institute on the use of the library of Congress classification* (1966: New York). Proceedings. Chicago: ALA, 1968, pp. 135-161.

119 2) Denisn, Barbara. Selected material in classification: A Bibliography. New York, N.Y.: Special Library Association, 1968. 142p.
Book numbers on page 2. It is a bibliography of 10 items mostly pertaining to local book number practices of some American University libraries.

120 3) Holmes, Robert ": Assignment of author numbers". In: *The use of Library of Congress classification: Proceedings of the Institute on the use of Library of Congress classification* edited by Richard H. Schimmelpfeng and C. Donald Cook. Chicago: ALA, 1968, pp. 107-120.

1969

121 1) Akers, Susan Grey: *Simple library cataloging*. 5th ed. Metuchen, N.J. The Scarecrow Press, 1969. pp. 31-34.

122 2) C.A. Cutter's three-figure author table. Swanson-Swift revision, 1969. Chicopee, Massa: H.R. Huntting Co, 1969. 29pp. 39x29 cm. Now distributed by Libraries Unlimited, Littleton, Colo).

123 3) C.A. Cutter's two-figure author table. Swanson-Swift revision, 1969. Chicopee, Mass: H.R. Huntting Co, 1969. 4pp. 36x22 cm. Now distributed by Libraries unlimited, Littleton, Colo.

124 4) Cutter, C.A.: "Another plan for numbering books". In: Rowland, A.R. Ed: *catalog and cataloging*. London: Crosby Lockwood, 1969, pp. 269-275.

125 5) Cutter-Sanborn three-figure author table. Swanson-Swift revision, 1969. Chicopee, Mass: H.R. Hutting Co. 1969. 33pp. 39x22 cm. (Now distributed by Libraries Unlimited, Littleton, Colo).

126 6) Levy, Grace. "Cuttering the corporate entry". *Spl Libraries* 60 (Dec 1969): 657-658.

1970

127 1) *Mauri, T: "Application of chrnological table for book numbers". (Japanese). Toshakan-Kai 22 (1) 1970: 32-40.

1971

128 1) Immroth, John Phillip: A guide to Library of Congress Classification. 2nd ed. Littleton, Colo: Libraries Unlimited, 1971. Book numbers pp. 38-42; 48-49 and 66-78. A new edition (1980) revised by Professor Lois Mai Chan is available.

129 2) Sengupta, B. and Ohdedar A.K.: *Library classification*. Culcutta: The World Press, 1971. p. 187 (deals in brief with Rider's book number).

1972

130 1) C.A. Cutter's three-figure alfabetic order table. "Fully rev. ed". Jammu, India: Light and Life Publisiers (1972 ?) 26p.

131 2) Cutter, C.A.: Cutter-Sanborn three-figure author table rev.ed. Ludhiana, India: Indian Bibliographical Centre, 1972, II, 40p. (Mimeographed).

132 3) Roy, J.B.: "A plan for modification of Cutter's author marks". *Iaslic Bulletin* 17(4) Dec 1972: 224-231.

1973

133 1) Higenbottom, Frank: *Codes and Ciphers*. Londn: St. Paul's House, 1973.

1974

134 1) Goil, N.K.: "From BN to ISBN". *Lib. Herald* 15(3-4) Oct 1973 March 1974: 151-167.

135 2) Makkar, G.C.: Three number author table. New Delhi: Today & Tomorrow's Printers and Publishers, 1974, xiv, 118p. A new table for author numbers. Adds facets of Colon book numbers to an alphabetical author table.

136 3) Sengupta, Benoyendra: *Cataloguing its theory and practice*. 3rd ed. Calcutta: The World Press, 1974. pp. 188-193. Deals with functions of book numbers; construction of CC book number has been given with some details.

1975

137 1) Bhargava, G.D. and Sod, S.P.: *Colon Classification: theory and practice*. Ujjain, Vijay Prakashan, 1975. pp. 82-88.

Obviously deals with Colon book numbers.

138 2) Coffmann, E.: "Man and/or machine: mind over matter". *W.Y.O. Library Roundup* 30 (1975): 11-12.

139 3) *Lehnus, Donald J: *Signatures libristicas: normas para su apliacacion en bibliotecas de habla hispana*. Reo Piedras, Puerto Rico: Editorial Universidad de Puerto Rico, 1975. In Spanish language.

140 4) Uppal, O.P.: *Practical procedure of classification*. Patiala: Madan Publishers, 1975. pp. 32-36. Gives a brief account of CC book number.

1976

141 1) Comaromi, John P: *The eighteen editions of the Dewey Decimal Classification*. Albany, N.Y.: Forest Press, 1976, pp. 99-106; 183-184. Gives a brief account of the origin of book numbers. An authentic account of (and source for) the history of book numbers.

142 2) Dowell, A.T.: "Classification and call numbers". In her: *Cataloguing with copy*. Littleton, Colo: Libraries Unlimited, 1976, pp. 135-199.

143 3) Mittal, R.L.: "Call number and collection number: their implications on book arrangement". *Indian library movement* 3(1) (1976): 1-6.

144 4) "Some cases of wrong Library of Congress card numbers being printed in books". *Unabashed Librarian* 20 1976: 18.

1977

145 1) La Trobe University Library. Technical Services Division. *Book numbers guide*. Bundoora, Australia : The Library, 1977.

146 2) Tiwari, P.C.: "Book numbers in theory and practice". *Herald of lib sc* 16(1) (January 1977): 49-51.

1978

147 1) Herdmann, Margaret M: *Classification: an introductory manual*, 3rd ed. rev by Jeanne Osborn. Chicago: ALA 1978, Book Numbers, pp. 28-38.

148 2) *Lehnus, Donald J: *Notacaode autor: manual para bibliotecas*. Traducaoe adaptacao de Hagar Espanha Gomes. Rio de Janeiro: BNG/Brasilart, 1978

1979

149 1) Carter, Ruth C: "Shelflist". In: *Encyclopaedia of Library & Information Science*, ed by Allen Kent, *et al*. New York: Marcel Dekker, 1979, Vol. 34, p. 334.

150 2) Satija, M.P.: *An epistle to Dean Shera on the brevity of notation in colon classification*. Amritsar: Rajat Book Corner, 1979, pp. 51-55. Deals with inherent structural provisions in the facet formula of the colon book number to make the colon book number brief in notational length.

151 3) Shukla, M.M.: "Book numbers". In: Venkatappiah, V, Subba Rao, C.V. and Chatterjee, Amitabha *Eds: March of library science: Kaula festschrift*. Delhi: Vikas Publishing House, 1979, pp. 169-178.

1980

152 1) Lehnus, Donald J.: *Book numbers: history, principles and application*. Chi-

cago: American Library Association, 1980. 153p.
After Barden (1937) a major book on the subject. Source for an informal and intimate history of book numbers with special reference to the development of Cutter tables.

153 2) *Richter, V: "The structure of the location mark". Struktura signatury. *Techn. Knih* 24 (1980): 193-201.
In Czechslovakian language.

154 3) Sachdeva, M.S.: *Colon Classification: theory and practice.* 2nd ed. New Delhi: Sterling Publishers, 1980. pp. 170-178. A lucid account of the mechanism of CC book number.

1981

155 1) Bavakutty, M: *Canons of Library classification.* Trivandrum: Kerala Library Association, 1981, pp. 116-136.

156 2) Chan, Lois Mai: *Cataloging and Classificaton: an introduction.* New York: McGraw-Hill, 1981. pp. 258-265; 286-291; 301-302 and 369-374.
A brief account of various author tables including the LC practice.

157 3) Comaromi, John P: *Book numbers: A historical study and practical guide to their use.* Littleton, Colo: Libraries Unlimited, 1981. 145p.
An important and authentic book giving a general account of various book numbers expecially the author tables and Biscoe's method. Studies various problems in book numbers. Its account of LC procedure is detailed and authentic.

1982

158 1) Library of Congress: "Author number: Library of Congress author number table". *LC Cataloguing Service Bulletin* Vol. 104, May 1982: 7-8

159 2) Osborn, Jeanne: *Dewey decimal classification, 19th ed: a study manual.* Littleton, Colo: Libraries Unlimited, 1982. Book Numbers, pp. 336-338.

1983

160 1) Krishan Kumar: *Theory of classification.* 3rd ed. New Delhi: Vikas Publishing House, 1983: pp. 340-352.
A brief account of major schemes of book numbers with emphasis on CC book numbers.

1984

161 1) Chand, M.P.: *Colon Classification: its structure and working.* Assisted by B.R. Sachdeva. 2nd ed. New Delhi: Sterling Publishers, 1984. pp. 128-132.
A brief account of Colon book number.

162 2) Raju, A.A.N: *Decimal, Universal decimal and Colon Classifications: a study in comparison.* New Delhi: Ajanta Publications, 1984. pp. 143-150.
Deals with CC book numbers.

163 3) Satija, M.P.: *Manual of practical colon classification.* New Delhi: Sterling Publishers, 1984. Book numbers, pp. 79-95.

164 4) Chand, Mahinder Partap. "Book numbers in Colon Classification". *ILA Bulletin* 20 (3-4) Oct 1984 - March 1985: 156-159.

1985

165 1) Dahlberg, I, *Comp & Ed. International classification and indexing bibliography*. Frankfurt: Indeks Verlag, 1985. Vol. 3, pp. 80-81 Sec 265. Contains a small bibliography of 12 references on book numbers.

166 2) Kaula, P.N.: *A treatise on Colon Classification*. New Delhi: Sterling Publishers, 1985, pp. 121-128.

167 3) Wynar, Bohdan S: *Introduction to cataloging and classification*. 7th ed. by Arlene G. Taylor. Littleton, Colo: Libraries Unlimited, 1985. pp. 426-435.

1986

168 1) Khanna, J.K.: *Colon classification: enumerated and expanded schedules*... New Delhi: Ess Ess Publications, 1986. pp. 109-120.

169 2) Library of Congress: *Subject cataloguing Division: Subject Cataloguing Manual Shelflisting*. Washington: The author, 1986. Various paging. It is a cumulation of all LC shelflisting rules and practices, and so renders Comaromi's work of historic interest only.

1987

170 1) Ranganathan, S.R.: *Colon classification*, 7th ed; edited by M.A. Gopinath. Bangalore: Sarada Ranganathan Endowment, 1987. Chap. CC, pp. 22-27.
It contains the latest version of the Ranganathan's book number.

171 2) Salvi, G.N. and Balakrishnan, M.R.: "Book numbering system in BARC library". *Iaslic Bull.* 32(1) 1987:1-10.

172 3) Satija, M.P.: "Book numbers: a reviewing article". *Int. classif.* 14(1) 1987: 44-46.

173 4) Satija, M.P.: "History of book numbers". *Int. classif.* 14(2) 1987: 70-76.

174 5) Satija, M.P.: *A primer on Ranganathan's book numbers*. Delhi: Mittal Publications, 1987. x, 87p. ISBN, 81-7099-004-1.

1988

175 1) Piggott, Mary: "Sub-arrangement by book numbers", pp. 180-182 of her, *A typography of cataloguing*. London: Library Association, 1988, 287p.

1989

176 1) Dhyani, Pushpa: *Classification schemes and Indian libraries*, 2nd rev ed. New Delhi: Metropolitan, 1989, pp. 177-179.
Studies variations in the book number used by libraries under survey.

177 2) Satija, M.P.: *Colon classification, 7th ed: a practical introduction*. New Delhi: Ess Ess Publications, 1989, Chap 8, pp. 103-118.

1990

178 1) Mishra, Sanjaya: "Colon book number" *Lucknow librarian* 22(3-4) 1990: 68-74

179 2) Satija, M.P.: "Book number and call number" *Encyclopaedia of library and information science*, edited by Allen Kent. New York: Marcel Dekker, 1990, Vol. 45, pp. 18-45.

180 3) Satija, M.P. and Agarwal, S.P.: *Book numbers: some Indian methods*. New Delhi: Concept Publishing Co, 1990. p. 96 ISBN. 81-7022-238-9

1991

181 1) Drabenstott, Karen M.: "Shelflisting using expert systems" In: International Study Conference on Classification Research (5th: 1991: Toronto). Paper.

Author Index to the Bibliography

SUBJECT INDEX

The chronology and the bibliography have not been indexed